D0988854

THE BEST

of

IRISH

HUMOR

THE BEST OF IRISH HUMOR

THE BEST

OF

IRISH HUMOR

A SUPERB COLLECTION OF HILARIOUS IRISH JOKES AND LIMERICKS

Edited by Marcia Kamien

Cover by Carol Russo Design

PLATINUM PRESS, LLC

2014

[3]

ISBN 978-1-879582-65-1

Printed and bound in the United States of America

First Edition

987654321

contents

THE BEST OF IRISH HUMOR

What it means to be Irish

- You will never play pro basketball.
- You swear very well.
- At least one of your cousins is a cop, firefighter, bar owner, funeral home owner, or is a politician.
- You spent a good deal of your childhood on your knees in prayer.
- You think you sing very well.
- You have no idea how to make a long story short.
- Much of your childhood meals were boiled.
- You will be punched for no good reason—a lot.
- Some of those punches are legacies from previous generations.
- You will have sisters or cousins named Mary, Eileen, Catherine or Colleen. Probably one of them is named Mary Eileen Catherine Colleen.
- If you don't know Murph, you know Mac and if you don't know Mac you know Sully. Maybe you know Sully MacMurphy.
- You are genetically unable to keep a secret.
- There wasn't a huge difference between your last wake and your last keg party.
- You're strangely poetic after a drink or two.
- You may not know the words, but you WILL sing.
- You have Irish Alzheimer's—you only remember the grudges.

THE BEST OF IRISH HUMOR

THE LUCK (AND BRAINS) OF THE IRISH

THE BEST OF IRISH HUMOR

A passerby watched two Donegal men in a park. One was digging holes and the other, right behind him, filling in the hole again. "What on earth are you doing?" asked the passerby. "Well," said the digger, "Usually there are three of us. I dig, Fergus plants and Liam fills in the hole. Fergus is unwell and can't work. But that don't mean Liam and I have to take the day off, does it?"

Soon after O'Leary clocked in for work, the foreman called him over and told him that he had a phone call in the front office. When O'Leary came back, he looked mournful. His foreman asked if it was bad news. "To be sure, it was. I just found out that my mother died this morning." "Gosh, that's awful," said the foreman. "Do you want the rest of the day off?" "No," said O'Leary, "I'll finish the day out." About an hour later, there was another call and when he came back, he looked terrible.. "Bejeezus, Boss, it's even worse. "That was my brother. "His mother died today, too!"

O'Malley and Maguire watch as a lorry goes by loaded with rolls of turf.
I'm gonna do that when I win the lottery, says O'Malley. Send me lawn out to be cut.

I met my friend Harrigan the other day and I said to him, "You look like a happy man."
He said, "That I am."
I said, "Why?"
"Well," he said, "the income tax people have been after me for 20 years, driving me mad, trying to get money out of me. But this morning I got a letter from them and it was stamped: FINAL NOTICE.
"Thank God," he said, "I won't be hearing from them again."

Pat and Mike were walking near a pub where an IRA bomb had exploded minutes before. Out of the smoldering ruins, a head rolled right past them.
Pat said, "Sure now, Mike, isn't that Jim Flannery?" Said Mike, "Nah, that couldn't be Jim Flannery.
"He was much taller than that."

It was the Christmas season and the teacher asked young Dennis Clancy, "What do you do at Christmastime?"

"Me and my brothers and sisters go to midnight mass; then we come home and put mince pies by the door and go to bed, waiting for Father Christmas to come with toys for us."

"And how about you, Annie Murphy?"

"Well, me and my sister also go to church and we sing carols and stay up late. We hang up our stockings and go to bed waiting for Santa Claus."

Realizing there was a Jewish boy in the class and not wanting to leave him out, she said, "Now, Jimmy Cohen, what do you do at Christmas?"

"It's the same every year. Dad comes home from the office. We all pile into the car and drive to his toy factory.

When we get inside, we look at all the empty shelves and we sing, 'What a friend we have in Jesus.'

"Then we all go to the Bahamas."

O'Toole was sitting in Ward's Irish bar, Piccadilly, London, with a large Rottweiler at his feet. "Does your dog bite?" says Doolittle. "No," says O'Toole.
So Doolittle reaches down to pat the dog, which nearly tears off his arm.
"Hey!" screams Doolittle. "You said your dog doesn't bite, O'Toole!"
Says O'Toole, "That's not my dog."

Paddy was trapped in a bog and seemed a goner when Big Mick Riley wandered by.
"Help!" Paddy shouted. "I'm sinkin'!"
"Don't you worry," said Mick. "Next to the Strong Muldoon, I'm the strongest man in Ireland and I'll pull ye right out of there."
Mick leaned out and grabbed Paddy's hands and pulled and pulled to no avail.
After two more unsuccessful attempts, Mick said, "Sure, and I can't do it. The Strong Muldoon could do it alone, mebbe, but I'll have to go get some help."
As Mick turned to leave, Paddy called, "Mick! D'ye think it will help if I pull me feet out of the stirrups?"

Two Irishmen meet and one says to the other, "Have ye seen Mulligan lately, Pat?" Says Pat, "Well, I have and I haven't."
"Sure, and what d'ye mean by that?"
Pat says, "It's like this, y'see...I saw a chap who I thought was Mulligan and he saw a chap he thought was me.
"But when we got close to each other... it was neither of us!"

Halligan and his wife are in bed one night and they hear the neighbor's dog is barking his head off in the garden. Disturbed by the noise, Halligan explodes: "Botheration and that!" and storms off downstairs.
He comes back upstairs five minutes later and his wife asks, "What did you do, Halligan?" He replies with a big grin. "I've put the dog in our garden, so I have. Now let's see how *they* like it!"

She was knitting and speeding and oblivious to the lights and sirens of the police car. So the policeman pulled next to her and yelled: "PULL OVER!"
"NO," she yelled back. "It's a SCARF!"

Gallagher is visiting Boston and is waiting patiently to cross the street.
The cop stops the flow of traffic and shouts, "Okay, pedestrians!" A few minutes later, he allows the traffic to pass. He does this a few times and Gallagher is still standing on the sidewalk. After the cop has shouted "Okay, pedestrians!" for the tenth time, Gallagher approaches him and says,
"Is it not about time ye let the Catholics across?"

Three good friends are stumbling home from the local pub late one night on the path through the graveyard.
"Come have a look here," says Michael. "It's Jim Flynn's grave, God bless his soul. He lived to the ripe old age of 87."
"That's nothing," says Padraic. "Here's one named Sean O'Boyle and it says he was 95 when he died." Just then, Sweeny yells out, "Good God, here's a fella that got to be 145!""What was his name?"
Sweeny squints a bit, then lights a match, looks closely, and exclaims, "Miles, from Dublin!"

A small boy came home from school in tears. "What's the matter, son?" asked his mother. "We were learnin' sums today, Mammy." "And were they too hard?" He said, "The teacher said either I can't count or I'm stupid, or all three."

I was traveling in County Mayo late one evening and stopped outside a little boarding house. I knocked on the door and a second later, the top floor window opened and a woman yelled down, "What do you want so late in the evening?"
I asked, "Could I stay here for the night?"
The woman yelled down to me, "YES!" and then slammed the window shut.

A woman gets on the bus to Belfast with her baby. As she pays for her ticket, the bus driver says, "That's the ugliest baby I've ever seen." The woman takes her seat, fuming. She says to the man next to her, "The driver just insulted me."
The man says, "You shouldn't have to take that. You go tell him off. I'll hold your monkey."

[17]

A lovely woman from County Clare died. She found herself outside a beautiful garden with splashing fountains and bright flowers; but she was alone and the gate was locked. When St. Peter finally came by, the woman said to him, "This is surely a wonderful place. It must be heaven. How do I get in?" "You have to spell a word," said the saint. "What word might that be?" "Love," said he. Well, she spelled it all right and was admitted through the Gates of Heaven.

About a year later, St. Peter asked this woman if she would mind guarding the Gates a short while for him. While she was waiting, her husband arrived. "How've you been?" she asked. "Oh, not bad," he said. "I married the pretty nurse who took care of you, and then I won the lottery. I sold our little cottage and bought a lovely mansion. My wife and I traveled 'round the world. Today I was skiing and broke my neck and...here I am. How do I get in?" "You have to spell a word." "What word?" "Czechoslovakia."

O'Connor won the Irish Sweepstakes and took a long holiday in America.
He went on a bus tour and travelled for many hours through desert country, with the occasional cactus and the occasional oil field.
O'Conner asked the guide, "Where in the world are we now?"
The guide said, "We're in the great state of Texas."
"It's a big place," O'Conner remarked.
The guide said, "It's so big that your County Kerry would fit right into the smallest corner of it."
O'Conner answered,
"Yes, and wouldn't it do wonders for it."

Finegan opened the morning newspaper and was dumbfounded to read in the obituary column that he had died.
 He quickly called his best friend, Ryan.
"Did you see the newspaper?" asked Finegan. "They said that I died."
"I saw it," replied Ryan.
 "Where ya callin' from?"

Riley applied for a job based in Belfast. An American applied for the same job. Since they both had the same qualifications, they were asked to take the same test. Upon completion, both men only missed one of the questions.

The manager said to Riley, "Thanks very much for your interest, but we're giving the job to the American."

Riley said, "Now, why would you be doing that? We both got all but one question right. And me being Irish and this being Ireland, I feel I should get the job over him."

Said the manager: "Our decision rests with the one question you both missed."

"And how could one wrong answer be better?"

"Simple," said the manager. "The American put down on question number thirteen, 'I don't know.' "You wrote, 'Neither do I.'"

His wife had been killed in an accident. "Did she say anything before she died?" asked the priest. "She talked without interruption for 40 years," said he.

Says Flanagan: " My wife has a terrible habit of staying up 'til 2:00 in the mornin'. I can't seem to break her of it." Says Hannigan: "What on earth is she doin', that hour of the mornin'?" Says Flanagan:
"Waitin' for me to come home."

A Scotsman, an Englishman and an Irishman find a wizard on top of a tall cliff. The wizard orders them to jump off the cliff but he also says that if they say anything while falling, they'll find that very thing at the bottom. The Englishman goes first and shouts, "Pillows!" and lands on a soft pile of pillows. Emboldened, the Scotsman jumps and shouts, "Hay!" and comes to rest of a giant pile of hay. Finally, the Irish runs to jump off the cliff, but he trips on a rock just before the jump and shouts, "Aw crap!"

An Irishman is speeding down a narrow hilly road, when a small car with a woman at the wheel comes hurtling around the corner, narrowly missing him. "Pig!" she shouts. The man turns and yells back "Bitch!" as he reaches the bend and crashes into a pig.

I first met Riley in an English hospital, lying in the bed next to me swathed in bandages from head to toe, just two little slits for his eyes. This made it somewhat difficult to engage him in conversation.

However, later that day his best friend, Callahan, came in to visit and I listened in to their conversation.

"What happened to you, Riley?"

"I drank a wee bit too much stout and staggered out of the Invincible Pub, where a lorry hit me a glancing blow and knocked me clear through the co-op's plate glass window. Broke it to smithereens, I did."

"Begorrah, it's a good job you were wearing all those bandages, or you would have been cut to ribbons!"

At the height of the Gulf Wars, the expertise of the well-known Irish fire-fighter Red Adair was called upon to go out to the battle and put out the oil rig fires, which were raging. On his way, his plane landed in Ireland for an overnight stop, so Red took advantage to visit the local for a pint of the black stuff.

When he came in, two old Irish boys saw him and one said to the other, "Isn't that Red Adair?"

"No," said his companion.

"Well, and I'm sure it is; and I'm so sure that I will bet you a pint if I'm wrong." The doubting one agreed and then both went over to Red and the one said, "Are you Red Adair?" To which Red said yes, he was. The doubting Irishman said, "Are you still dancing with Ginger Rogers?"

Flanigan and Murphy are working on a building site. Flanigan says to Murphy, "I want a day off. I'm gonna pretend I'm mad!" He climbs up to the rafter, hangs upside down and shouts, "I'M A LIGHTBULB! I'M A LIGHTBULB!"

Murphy watches in amazement; and sure enough, the foreman shouts, "Flanigan, you're mad, go home." Flanigan leaves the site. Murphy immediately starts packing his kit up to leave as well.

"Where the hell are you going?" demands the foreman. "I can't work in the friggin' dark!" says Murphy.

John Branford, a Dublin University student, was on the side of the road hitchhiking. It was a very dark and stormy night and, sure enough, there were no cars passing by. Then suddenly, he saw a car slowly coming toward him. It stopped. John instantly got into the car and closed the door...only to find there was nobody behind the wheel and the engine wasn't on. Terrified, John hunkered into his corner, praying for his life.

The car continued to move very slowly and when a bend appeared in the road and he was certain he would die, a hand out of nowhere came though the driver's window and turned the wheel, then disappeared. Now John was TRULY frightened.

Soon, John saw the lights of a pub appear through the sheets of rain and without further thought, he jumped out of the car and ran to the pub.

Wet through and out of breath, he rushed inside and started telling everyone about the ghost car. A silence enveloped the pub when everybody realized he was crying and wasn't drunk.

Suddenly, the pub door opened and two other sopping wet men staggered in, panting and gasping for air.
Looking around and seeing John Branford sobbing at the bar, one said to the other, "Look, Paddy...there's that fooking idiot that got in the car while we were pushing it!"

An Englishman, a Scotsman and an Irishman were reading an article that said an Irishman's brain or a Scotsman's brain could be bought for 500 Euros but an Englishman's brain cost 10,000 Euros.
"That proves," said the Englishman, "that Englishmen are much cleverer than Irishmen or Scotsmen."
"No, it doesn't," said the Irishman. "It means an Englishman's brain has never been used."

A turtle in Ballyvaughn was attacked by a pack of snails.
When the Garda questioned him, he said, "It all happened too fast!"

Three Irish fellas go to an Irish pub in Boston, have a few pints, then ask for their tab. The bar-back brings them a bill for exactly $30. Each gives him a tenner and they prepare to leave.

Then the bartender tells the bar back that the bill was only $25 and hands him a five-dollar bill to give them.

They're halfway out the door and the bar back thinks, I work hard, I deserve something; so he gets five $1 bills, keeps two and gives each of the customers $1.

So far, so good.

$30 minus $5 = $25, right?

$5 minus $3 = $2. All is well, right?

Not quite.

So what's the problem?

Figure this out:

Each of the 3 guys gave $10. Each got back $1.

That means they paid $9 each for their beer, which times 3 is $27.

The bar back kept $2 for himself.

$27 plus $2 = $29.

All right, then, tell me this:

Where the heck is the other dollar?

Micky was taking a walk in the country. In a field he saw something intriguing. Why didn't that cow have horns? He spotted the farmer, who was planting and walked over to ask him.

The farmer stood up, stretched his back, and said, "We keep their horns trimmed back with a hacksaw. We can also treat calves so their horns don't grow. And some breeds just don't have horns at all.

"But as for this cow that you're lookin' at. She doesn't have horns because she's a horse!"

There was an old lady of Harrow
Whose views were exceedingly narrow.
At the end of her paths
She built two bird baths
For the different sexes of sparrow.

There was a young lady of Torrence
Who for kissing professed great abhorrance.
But when she'd been kissed
And found out what she'd missed,
She cried 'til her tears came in torrents.

A naïve young lady of Bude
Had not seen a man in the nude.
When a lewd fellow showed
His all on the road
She did not know *what* to conclude!

An epicure dining at Crewe
Found a rather large mouse in his stew.
Said the waiter, "Don't shout
And wave it about,
Or the rest will be wanting one, too."

An Irishman swore and averred
He had learned to fly like a bird.
Cheered by thousands of people
He leapt from the steeple.
His tomb states the date it occurred.

"A book and a jug and a dame,
And a nice cozy nook for the same.
And I don't give a damn,"
Said Omar Khayyam
"What you say. It's a great little game."

How do most Irishmen define marriage?
A very expensive way of getting their
laundry done for them.

In revolutionary Paris, 1789, three spies
from across the channel were about to be
guillotined.
"Do you want to be on your back or your
front?" asked the executioner of Smith.
"On my back," said Smith. "I'm not afraid to
die."
The executioner pulled the lever... and the
blade jammed.
Smith was reprieved because no man can be
sentenced to death twice.
Sinclair was next and he, too, chose to face
the knife.
Once again, the blade jammed and Sinclair
was set free.
When Murphy was asked, he said, "I'll do
same as the others."
So he was laid on his back under the blade.
"Begorrah," he shouted.
"Stop! Just a minute. I think I can see why
it jams!"

Father O'Malley looked out his window one morning and saw a jackass lying dead in the front garden.

He promptly called Sgt. Flaherty at the police station. "This is Father O'Malley. There's a jackass lying dead in my front garden. Could you be sending a couple of your lads to see to the matter?"

"Well, now, Father, I thought you people always took care of the last rites."

"Aye, that's right. But we are obliged to notify the next of kin."

Clancy and Carey went into a chocolate store. But they had no money, so they soon left. Outside, Clancy said to Carey, "I'm the best thief in County Mayo. I stole three chocolate bars and the owner never twigged. You can't beat that."

"Oh, really? I think I can. I'll steal three bars of chocolate while the owner is looking at me."

They go back in and Carey says, Would you like to see a great magic trick?" "Shure and I would," says the shopkeeper.

Carey says, "Give me three of those chocolate bars."
And he proceeds to eat them, one after the other, smacking his lips with pleasure.
"But where's the magic?" demands the shopkeeper.
"Look in Clancy's pocket," says Carey.

An Irishman, an Englishman and a Scotsman all wanted to see the final rounds of the Irish Games; but they had no tickets. They circled the stadium and came upon a construction site. The Englishman grabbed a length of scaffolding, went to the gate and said, "Johnson. The pole vault."
He was let in.
The Scot thought this a grand idea and scouted until he found a sledge hammer. At the gate, he said, "McTavish, hammer throw," and was admitted.
The Irishman looked and looked and finally saw his ticket in.
 Seizing a roll of barbed wire, he presented himself at the gate and said, "O'Sullivan. Fencing."

Sean wakes up in the hospital, covered in bandages and hurting all over. His friend Seamus is sitting by the bed.
"What happened to me?" Sean groans.
"You had a few too many last night and you made a bet you could jump out the window and fly around the pub."
"Why in hell didn't you stop me?"
"Stop you?" says Seamus. "Hell, I bet twenty-five pounds on you!"

O'Leary tells me this: I'm starting to take this drink driving thing seriously now. Left the car in the pub car park last night and took the bus home.
Quite proud of meself, really. I've never driven a bus before.

There was a young lass from Kavan
Who was terribly sick in a train.
Not once, but again,
And again and again-
And again and again and again.

Magic 8-Ball: not good as pregnancy test.

Connery is run over by a bus on his way out of the pub. He finds himself at the gate to heaven and St. Peter tells him that, in order to get in, he'll have to pass a test.
Connery groans. He never was the brightest bulb in the box, but what choice does he have?
St. Peter decides to go easy on him. "What has five fingers and is made of leather?" he asks. Connery scratches his head, thinks hard and finally gives up.
"It's a glove," says St. Peter. "Let's try again. What has ten fingers and is made of leather? Think, now. This one is easy." But not to Connery, who is clearly stumped.
"Why, it's two gloves," says St. Peter. "Don't you see?" He holds up two hands. "Ten fingers, leather. Two hands, two gloves."
Connery will never pass a test, but St. Peter is in a generous mood. He'll give him the easiest question for an Irishman.
"Who is the patron saint of Ireland?"
"It wouldn't be three gloves, would it?" says Connery.

An American, a Japanese and an Irishman were sitting naked in the sauna. Suddenly something beeped. The American pressed his forearm and the beeping stopped. "That was my pager," he said. "I have a microchip under the skin of my arm."

A moment later, a phone rang. The Japanese fellow lifted his palm to his ear and had a short conversation. "That was my cellphone microchip."

Murphy the Irishman felt decidedly low-tech. He felt he had to do *something*. He stepped out of the sauna and went to the toilet. He returned with a piece of toilet paper hanging from his behind.

The other men raised eyebrows. "Will ya look at that!" said Murphy. "I'm getting a fax!"

An American was driving through County Clare when his motor stopped. He got out and lifted the hood to see if he could locate the problem.

A voice behind him said, in a heavy Irish brogue, "'Tis the carburetor."

He turned around to see an old horse standing by a fence.

The horse said again, "Ye should look to the carburetor."

The American nearly died of fright and dashed into the nearest pub, had a large whisky and told Murph the barkeep what had just happened.

"Oh, don't listen to him," Murph said. "He don't know nothin' about cars anyway."

A man from Wicklow took a photograph of his son to the chemist.

"I wonder," he said, "Could you enlarge this for me?"

"Yes, of course," the chemist replied.

"And could you take his hat off for me?"

"We could do something...touch it up for you. It wouldn't be perfect, but I think it would do the trick.

"Just tell me, which side does your son part his hair?"

The Wicklow man smiled.

"Surely you'll see that when you take his hat off."

A group of Americans was touring Ireland. One of the women was always complaining. *The food is terrible. It's too hot. It's too cold. The accomodations are awful.* The guide was becoming quite annoyed at this woman and her carping, but what could he do? She was a customer and a guest in Ireland, so he held his tongue.

One fine day, the group arrived at the site of the famous Blarney Stone.

"Good luck will be following you all your days if you kiss the Blarney Stone," said the guide. "Unfortunately, it's being cleaned today. Perhaps we can come back tomorrow."

Cried the nasty woman, "We won't be here tomorrow, remember? We have some other boring site to visit. So I guess we'll never be able to kiss the stupid stone."

"Well, now," said the guide, "'Tis said that if you kiss someone who has kissed the stone, you'll have the same good fortune."

"And I suppose," scoffed the woman, "that you have kissed the stone."

"No, ma'am," said he with a smile. "But I have sat on it."

There was an old maid from Duluth
Who wept when she thought of her youth,
And the glorious chances
She'd missed at school dances,
And once in a telephone booth.

Throughout the whole world experts say
That Geography rules...well, okay.
Though it's not the location
But the mere appellation
That's important down Limerick way.

There was a young lady from Pecking
Who indulged in a great deal of necking.
Which seemed such a waste,
Since she claimed to be chaste—
That statement, however, needs checking.

A lady there was in Antigua,
Who said to her spouse, "What a pig you
are!"
He answered, "My queen!
Is it my manner you mean?
Or do you refer to my figua?"

[37]

The local Garda was an unpleasant sort, and he was in a bad mood. He stopped a local farmer on a minor driving infraction and berated him for this and that. The farmer said nothing, not even when the Garda started writing him up. While he was writing, he kept swatting at the flies that were circling his head and buzzing at his ears.

"Them circle flies botherin' ya?"

"Why do ya call 'em circle flies, old man?"

"We call 'em that on the farm because they're always circling around the horses' behinds."

"Say, old man, are you callin' me a horse's arse?" snarled the Garda.

"Oh, saints no," said the farmer. "I wouldn't think of such a thing."

The Garda kept writing and swatting.

"...Kinda hard to fool them flies, though."

A Texas rancher visits an Irish farm and sneers, "Takes me a day to drive from one end of my land to the other."

Retorts the Irish farmer, "We got tractors like that over here, too."

A man from Kildare was given the job of painting white lines down the middle of a road. On his first day, he painted eight miles; on his second day, he painted three miles and on his third day, he painted just one mile. The boss was not best pleased. "Why is it that you're painting less each day?" he demanded.

"Because each day I get further away from the can of paint."

At the pharmacy, Molly asked to use the infant scale to weigh the baby in her arms. The clerk explained that the infant scale was out for repairs; but explained that she could figure the infant's weight by weighing the two of them together on the adult scale, then holding the baby and weighing Molly alone and subtracting. "It won't work," Molly said. "I'm not the mother. I'm the aunt."

Two middle-aged ladies from Fordham
Went out for a walk and it bored 'em.
As they made their way back
A sex maniac
Leapt out from some trees and ignored 'em.

A man walking past a building site was surprised to see three big Irish labourers holding hands and dancing round a hole in the ground.

"What's this, then?" he asked the foreman. "Someone's birthday?"

"No," said the foreman, "it's the third anniversary of the hole."

A Belfast decorator was painting a house and the owner came home to find the man rushing about like a mad thing with his brushes.

"Why are you working so fast?" he asked.

"Well, you see, sor, the paint's running low and I want to finish the job before it's all gone."

A Dubliner was charged with murder, and was acquitted by the skin of his teeth. Afterwards, he told his lawyer that he could prove he was innocent because he was in jail at the time. "Why on earth didn't you tell me that?' his lawyer asked.

"I thought it might prejudice the court against me."

During WWII, a German spy was trained to go to Ireland. "We need to keep an eye on what the Irish are doing," said his commander. "We will parachute you into Ireland, where you will go to the local town and ask for Murphy. He's your contact. You will say to him, 'The weather could change by Tuesday.'"

The German landed safely, buried his parachute and set off for the nearest town. On the way, he saw a farmer working. "Good day to ya," he said, quite sure that he sounded like a native. "Would you know where I could find Mr. Murphy?"

"Well, sir, it depends which Murphy you want. We have Dr. Murphy, Father Murphy, Murphy in the Post Office and, as a matter of fact, me own name is Murphy."

How will he ever find the right man? The German thought. They all have the same name. And then he had an idea.

"The weather could change by Tuesday," he said.

A smile spread across the farmer's face. "Ah, then," he said, "You'll be wanting Murphy the spy."

A man sees his doctor, saying he hurts everywhere. He prods himself in the torso, arms, and legs, complaining each time.
"Are you Irish?" asks the doctor.
"Yes," says the patient.
"I thought so. Your finger is broken."

Two Irish mothers, Kate and Lorna were talking about their sons.
Kate says, "My Patrick is such a saint. He works hard, doesn't smoke, and he hasn't so much as looked at a woman in two years."
Lorna retorts, "Well, my Francis is pretty much of a saint himself. Not only hasn't he not looked at a woman in over three years, but he hasn't touched a drop of liquor in all that time."
"My word," says Kate. "You must be so proud."
"That I am," says Lorna. "And when he's paroled next month, I'm going to throw him a big party."

Says Seamus: if the other driver had stopped a few yards behind himself the accident would not have happened.

Murphy's wife took the car to the supermarket and as she came out laden with groceries, she saw a lad break into the car, hot wire it, and drive off. Naturally, she reported the incident to the police. "What did he look like?" asked the officer. "I don't really know," she said, "but I got the license plate number."

An Irishman, Kevin by name, and an American, Clint, are sitting at the bar in Cork Airport, drinking Guinness.
"I've come to meet my brother," says Kevin. "He's due to fly in from Boston in an hour's time. It's his first trip home in forty years."
"Do you think you'll recognize him?"
"I'm sure I won't," says Kevin. "He's been gone a long time and I'm sure he's changed."
"Well, then," says Clint, "I wonder if he'll recognize you."
"Of course he will. Sure, and I haven't been away at all!"

When they tell you St. Patrick drove out all the snakes, do they say only he saw them?

[43]

A very pregnant Irish woman from O'Dowd is in a car accident and falls into a coma. Comatose for four months, when she wakes up and realizes what has happened, she frantically asks her doctor about her baby. "Don't you be worrying yourself," says the doctor. "We delivered you of a fine set of twins, boy and girl; and they're home with a baby nurse. You'll see them soon."
"And what did my husband call them?"
"Oh, he was out of the country, so your brother from Kildare named them."
"Oh, no!" thinks the woman, "Not my stupid brother." With trepidation, she asks the doctor, "What did he call them?"
"The girl is Denise."
"Well, that's not a bad name, not at all. And the boy?"
"Denephew."

His daughter's wedding was a week away and Heffernan still didn't know what he was going to say in his reception speech. He went to the pub and asked Sullivan's advice. Sullivan said, "I think you should talk about ... um ... two minutes."

There now follows a list of inventions from the unluckiest fellow in Donegal. Over the years he came up with sodas called 4-Up, 5-Up, and 6-Up. None of them did well, so he gave up and someone else made the fortune with you-know-what.
And if that wasn't bad enough, look at these other things he thought up:
*an inflatable dartboard
*a chocolate kettle
*a soluble life raft
*a solar-powered flashlight

An Irishman, an Englishman and a German are caught in Saudi Arabia, drinking. Under Saudi law, they each must get 30 lashes and deportation.
The Englishman is asked what he would like on his back before the lashing and he asks for linseed oil—which doesn't help much.
The German says he wants nothing and he limps off slowly, cursing.
The Irishman is asked by the guards what he would like on his back before his lashing. "Oh," replies the Irishman, "I'll have the German."

EXAM TO BECOME AN HONORARY IRISHMAN

Instructions to candidates

- a) Do not attempt to answer more than one question at a time.
- b) Do not attempt to write on both sides of the paper at the same time.
- c) On no account attempt Question 3.
- d) Slide rules okay.

NB Candidates caught cheating will be given extra marks for initiative. All candidates are requested to use separate answer books.

Time allowed: 6 weeks

....

1. Who won the Second World War? Who came in second?
2. Explain in one sentence Einstein's Theory of Relativity OR write your name in block capitals.
3. What is the number of this question?
4. Name the odd man out: The Chief Rabbi, the Pope, Jack the Ripper, the Archbishop of Canterbury.

[46]

5. At the Irish Sheepdog Trial of 1972, how many sheepdogs were found guilty?

6. At what time is the 9 o'clock news?

7. Spell each of the following words: DOG, CAT, PIG.

8. Write a tongue twister three times quickly.

9. There have been six kings of England named George. The last was George the Sixth. Name the other five.

A man walked into a bar in Belfast.
He saw a lovely, smartly-dressed woman perched on a bar stool. Approaching her, he said, "Hello, there, gorgeous. How are you?"
Having already had more than a few power drinks, she turned around, looked him straight in the eye and announced, "Listen! I'll screw anybody, any time, anywhere, my place, your place, front door, back door, it doesn't matter to me!"
Eyes wide, he said, "No kidding? I'm a lawyer, too. What firm are you with?"

A construction site boss is interviewing men for a job, when along comes Murphy. The boss thinks, "I'm not hiring that lazy Mick" and he decides to ask Murphy questions he couldn't possibly answer.

The first question: without using numbers, represent the number 9. Murphy answers by drawing three trees. The boss says, "What's <u>that?</u>" Murphy says "Tree and tree and tree makes nine." "So now, under the same rules show me 99." Murphy thinks for a minute, then makes a smudge on each tree. The boss says, "How in the devil does that say 99?" Murphy says, "Each tree is dirty. Dirty tree and dirty tree and dirty tree, dat's 99." The boss is getting worried he may have to hire this guy, so he says, "Same rules again and the number I want is 100." Murphy stares into space, then smiles. He makes a little mark at the base of each tree. "There ya go, sir. 100." A little dog comes along and craps by each tree. Ya got dirty tree an' a turd, and dirty tree and a turd, and dirty tree and a turd, which adds up to a hundred, when do I start my job?"

Mick died in a fire and was badly burnt. So the morgue needed someone to identify the body. His two best friends, Seamus and Murph were sent for.

Seamus said, "Yup, he's burnt pretty bad. Roll him over, wouldya?"

The mortician rolled the body over. "Nope," said Seamus. "Not Mick."

Next, Murph came in, looked and said, "No, that ain't Mick."

The mortician said, "How can you tell?"

Murph said, "Well, ya see, Mick had two arseholes."

"What? But that's impossible!"

"But everybody knew that. Every time the three of us went into town, folks would say, "Here comes Mick with them two arseholes."

Some strange auto insurance claims:

.To avoid a collision, I ran into the other car.

.A pedestrian hit me and went under my car.

.She suddenly saw me, lost her head and we met.

.Cow wandered in front of my car. I was told afterward that the cow is half-witted.

.A bull suddenly ran and gored my car.

Cassidy walked into the local welfare office to pick up his check. He marched straight up to the counter and said, "You know, I just HATE drawing welfare. I'd really rather have a job."

The social worker behind the counter said, "Your timing is excellent. We just got a job opening from a wealthy old man who wants a chauffeur and bodyguard for his beautiful daughter. You'll be expected to accompany his daughter on her overseas holday trips and you are warned that she's young and has a strong sex drive."

Cassidy gave the social worker a skeptical look. "Now you're bullshittin' me," he said. The social worker said, "Yeah, well ... you started it."

"It was just a simple misunderstanding, Your Honor," testified the man charged with indecent exposure.

"Explain that statement," said the judge. "Well, you see, this girl and I were drinking in a bar and she asked me what I wanted most in a woman.

"So I showed her."

Kelly walks into a pub and orders two single whiskies.

"Do you want them both now," asks the bartender, "or one at a time?"

"Oh, both now," says Kelly. "One's for me and one's for my little friend here."

He pulls a three-inch man out of his shirt pocket. The little guy slurps the whiskey.

"What else can he do?" asks the bartender. "Can he walk?"

"Sure, and he can." Kelly throws a coin down the bar and the little guy runs to retrieve it.

"Well, that's amazing," says the bartender. "Does he talk as well?"

"Of course," says Kelly. "Brian, tell him about that time we were in Africa and you called that witch doctor an asshole."

A writing class at Trinity was told to write a short story in as few words as possible, and containing religion, sex, and mystery.

One story got an A plus:

"Oh, God, I'm pregnant.

"I wonder who did it?"

Jimmy O'Leary was driving his lorry when he saw a bridge with a sign says "10 FOOT MAX." He slowed down, wondering if he could make it underneath. Agh, shure and I'll give it a go, he thought, only to find he got stuck halfway through.

Jimmy sat back in his seat, poured himself a cup of tea and lit a cigarette. A policeman arrived a short time later and knocked on the cab door. "What do you think you're doin'?" he said sharply.

"Shure, I'm havin' me tea break," said Jimmy.

"And what is it you work at?"

"Agh, shure, I deliver bridges," said Jimmy, with a big smile.

Seamus needed a raise and he wasn't getting one. He went to the boss and said, "Now you have to give me a rise. Otherwise, there are 3 companies after me." The boss said, "Oh, Really. Which ones?" "Telephone company, mortgage company, electricity company." The boss had a laugh and Seamus got his raise.

A wealthy businessman bought a mansion built on the edge of a cliff, overlooking a beautiful lake with cliffs on the other side. The view was spectacular and he took a walk each evening, to take in the sunset. One blustery night, he was blown clear off balance and fell off the edge.

On his way down, he grabbed onto a slender sapling growing out of the rock, trembling with fear.

Casting his eyes heavenward, he called out, "Is anyone there?"

At once a great voice came out of nowhere, saying: "Someone is always here, my son. Let go of the small tree and and you will descend safely to the shore below."

The man thought about this for a moment, then looked down at the jagged rocks below. Finally, he shouted: "Is there anyone else up there?"

O'Banion went to the Post Office and asked were there any letters for him. "Your name?" asked the clerk. "You're havin' me on," he said. "Sure, an' my name will be on the envelope, won't it?"

Upon seeing his son's black eye, Callahan asked how it happened. "It's the damnedest thing. I was at Molly's house dancin' with the lovely lass, when her father walked in."
"And did he think that dancin' is evil and that?"
"No, Da, he's deaf and couldn't hear the music."

Higgins was selling his house and decided to put the matter into an agent's hands.
When he saw the description of his house that the agent had written, he said,
"Begorrah, and is this all true, what's in me house?"
"Certainly," said the agent. "Every detail."
"Well, then," said Higgins, "Take it off your list. It's too good to give up."

Connery put his rifle underneath a pew and ran into the confessional. "Father," he said, "I've just shot two English lieutenants."
When there was no response, he went on, "Have ye fainted?" "No," said the confessor. "I'm waitin' for you to stop talking politics and commence confessin' your sins."

A little Protestant boy in Belfast was not doing well in school, particularly in math; and his parents were worried. He refused to study. They decided to send him to a Catholic school, where they heard the nuns were tough. Their son hadn't been at his new school for a week when his study habits took a turn for the better. Every day he came home and went to his homework first. His grades improved. So they asked him why he was doing so much better. Were the classes more interesting? No. Were the teachers more demanding? No. Why, then, had he improved so quickly?

"Well," said the boy, "on my first day at Our Lady of Perpetual Sorrows, I didn't pay much attention. It seemed just like any other school.

"Then I looked up and saw this naked guy nailed to a plus sign and I knew then that they really meant business!"

Two English ladies bemoaned all the Irish coming to their vacation spots. So Bridget said, "Go to Hell, why don't ye? There are no Irish there!"

Seamus and Sean were riding tandem on a bike when Sean cried out: "The wind is cuttin' into me chest somethin' fierce, Seamus!'

"We'll fix that" Seamus said. "Turn your jacket front to back and your chest will be protected from the wind."

Sean did that and pronounced himself much warmer. They got back on the bike and continued their ride.

After a bit, Seamus turned to talk to Sean and was horrified not to see his friend there. He turned the bike around immediately and went to see what had happened.

Not far down the road, he saw Sean sitting, surrounded by a group of farmers.

"T'anks be to heaven," he said. "Is he alright?"

"He was fine when we got here," said one of the farmers. "But since we turned his head back to front, he hasn't said a word."

How does a man save women from being attacked on the street at night?
He controls himself.

Three Englishmen were in a bar and spotted an Irishman. So one of the Brits walked over to him, tapped him on the shoulder and said, "Hey, I hear your St. Patrick was a drunken loser."

"Oh, really," came the response. "Hmmm. Didn't know that."

Puzzled, the Englishman walked back to his buddies. "I told him St. Patrick was a loser, and he didn't care."

The second Englishman said, "You just don't know how to set them off...watch and learn." He walked over to the Irishman, tapped him on the shoulder and said, "Hey, I hear your St. Patrick was lying, cheating, idiotic, low-life scum of the earth!"

"Oh, really, hmmm, didn't know that."

Shocked, the Englishman went back to his friends. "You're right, he's unshakable."

"Boys, I'll really tick him off...just watch," said the third Englishman.

He walked over to the Irishman, tapped him on the shoulder, and said, "I hear St. Patrick was really an Englishman."

"Indeed, that's what your buddies were tryin' to tell me."

Three guys, one Irish, one English, one Scottish are walking together on the beach one fine day. They come across an old tarnished oil lamp and when one of them picks it up, out pops a genie.

"I'll give three wishes in thanks," he says. "One for each of you."

The Scot says, "I'm a fisherman, my father and grandfather were fishermen, and my son will probably be a fisherman, too. I'll like all the oceans filled with fish for eternity."

Poof! it is as he wants: so many fish in the sea that they're washing up on the beach for lack of room.

The Englishman, amazed, says, "I want a big strong wall around England so we can never be conquered again."

Poof! in the distance they see a wall looming.

The Irishman says, "You're good, genie lad. So tell me about this wall."

"It's 500 meters high and 6 meters thick; nobody and nothing could get in or out."

"Lovely," says the Irishman.

"Now fill it with water."

Kathleen usually car-pooled with one of the other computer women at her company; but the other woman had called in sick, so she had to take a cab.

In the confusion of getting all her things together and making sure the lights were out and so on, she forgot her purse, which she kept for safety in her desk drawer.

She didn't realize this until the cab pulled up in front of her building.

"Och, I'm not belivin' I did this, sir, but I left me purse at the office. I'll not be able to pay you this minute but if you give me your card, I'll get it to you tomorrow morning."

The driver chuckled and said, "Now, Missy, never mind the money. I'll just pull up into that dark alley up there and get into the back with you and take off your panties."

Kathleen said, "Shure, and it's the bad end of the bargain you'll be getting'. Those panties only cost me eighty-nine cents."

The reasonable man adapts himself to the world; the unreasonable one persists in trying to adapt the world to himself.

-George Bernard Shaw

An English tourist asked Liam: "Could you tell me the way to Balbriggan, please?"
"Certainly, sor. If you take the first road to the left...no, still that wouldn't do...drive on for about four miles then turn left at the crossroad...no, that won't do either."
Liam scratched his head thoughtfully.
"You know, sor, if I was going to Balbriggan, I wouldn't start from here at all."

After digging to a depth of 300 feet last year, Russian scientists found traces of copper wire dating back 1000 years, and concluded that their ancestors had telephone lines one thousand years ago.
American scientists then dug down 600 feet and discovered traces of silica. Their headlines read: "Scientists find 2000-year-old optical fibers," and concluded that their ancestors had advanced digital phones long before the Russians.
A week later, Irish newspapers trumpeted the following story: "Scientists digging 1500 feet down have found nothing. Obviously, 5000 years ago, Ireland's ancestors already had wireless technology."

A truck breaks down in Manhattan with a cargo of 20 live chimpanzees bound for the Bronx Zoo. The driver knows he'll lose his job if he doesn't get the monkeys there on time. So he sweats and strains to fix his truck. Eventually, an Irish trucker pulls up. "Where are the monkeys going?
"Do me a favor and take these to the Bronx Zoo and I'll give you a hundred bucks."
"Happy days," says the Irishman. "No problem." He off-loads the monkeys into his truck and gets going.
A couple of hours later, the Irishman is back again, with all the chimps on board.
Panicked, the trucker flags him down.
"What are you playing at?" he fumes. "I told you to take them to the Bronx Zoo!"
"Begorrah and so I did," says the Irishman. "But we liked it so much and I had fifty bucks left, so we're going to Central Park."

"Got a cooking book for my birthday," says Kevin. "But I couldn't use it."
"Too many fancy recipes?" said Dennis.
"Couldn't get past the first line: "Take a clean dish…"

[61]

Three men, an Aussie, a Brit and an Irishman are stranded on a desert island. They find a dirty old bottle, rub it, and out pops a genie.
Three wishes are granted, one each.
The Aussie wants to go home. Poof! he's gone. The Brit wants to visit the Queen. Poof! he's gone.
The Irishman says, "Now I'm lonely. Wish they were here."

Murph went to see Riverdance when it toured Dublin. When he arrived at the theatre, the clerk in the box office asked, "And where would you like to sit, sir?"
"At the shallow end," replied Murph.

Danny O'Toole went into his bank. "I'd like to see someone about a loan," he said.
"I'm sorry, sir, but the loan arranger isn't here just now." "I'll have a word with Tonto then."

Long ago, when men cursed and beat the ground with sticks, it was witchcraft. Today, we call it golf.

[62]

Pat trained for the Dublin Marathon. For 6 weeks, he ran five miles a day. But at the end of six weeks he was 210 miles from the race.

"You promised to come yesterday to fix my doorbell," moaned the woman when O'Hara the handyman eventually turned up on her doorstep.
"I did come around yesterday," he said. "I rang the doorbell twice but got no answer."

Bridget was stopped by the Garda and asked if she could show them her driving license. Angrily, she snapped, "I wish you could make your minds up! Yesterday, you took away my license and today you want to see it!"

With Aer Lingus, you can have the experience of having breakfast in London, lunch in Dublin, dinner in Galway, and your luggage in Rome.

Most advice can be had for nothing—and usually it's worth it.

[63]

Dylan Riley had long heard stories of an amazing family tradition. His father, grandfather and great grandfather had all been able to walk on water on their 18th birthday. So when his 18th birthday came around, he and his mate Mick took a boat out into the middle of the lake. Dylan stepped out and nearly drowned and Mick just managed to haul him to safety.

Furious and confused, Dylan went to his grandmother. "Granny," he said. "'Tis me 18th birthday, so why can't I walk 'cross the lake like me father, his father and his father before him?"

Granny Riley looked deeply into Dylan's troubled eyes and said, "Because yer father, yer grandfather and yer great-grandfather were all born in December, when the lake is frozen, and you were born in August, ya bloody eejit!"

Aiden's friend Cormac got himself two new dogs and invited Aiden to come see them. "What d'you call them" said Aiden. "Timex and Rolex." "Odd names, aren't they?" "Well, they're watchdogs."

Two young Irishmen in a Canadian regiment were going into the trenches for the first time. Their Captain promised them 50 pence for every German they killed.
Pat lay down to rest and Mick kept watch.
Soon Mick shook Pat awake.
"They're comin'!"
"Who's comin'?"
"The Germans!"
"How many are there, d'ye think?"
"Around 50,000!"
""Begorrah," shouted Pat, grabbing his rifle and leaping up. "Our fortune's made!"

Three little boys in Galway were convinced that they needed to be baptized so they could go to Sunday School. They went to the nearest church. Only the custodian was there but he said he would "baptize" them. He took them to the bathroom, dunked their heads quickly in the toilet bowl one at a time, and said, "There ye go."
When they got outside, they wondered what religion they were. The littlest one said, "Can't you tell by the smell of that water what we are? We're Pisscopalians."

AN IRISH MOTHER'S LETTER TO HER SON

Dear Son, Just a few lines to let you know I am still alive. I am writing slowly because I know you cannot read very well.

It only rained twice last month. The first time was for three days and the second for four. On Monday the wind blew so hard that one of the chickens laid the same egg four times.

Your father has a grand new job, with 500 people under him. He cuts the grass at the graveyard.

Auntie Peggy has sent you a pair of socks she knitted for you. She put in a third one because she heard you've grown a foot since she last seen you.

That coat you asked me to send you: your Auntie Nora said it would be a little too heavy to send in the mail with those heavy buttons, so we cut them off and put them in the pockets.

There was a new style of washing machine in the house when we moved in, but it wasn't working too good. I put 14 shirts into it last week, pulled the chain, and I haven't seen them since!

Your sister Colleen had a baby this morning. I haven't found out yet whether it was a boy or a girl, so I don't know if you are an Uncle or an Aunt.

You won't recognize the house anymore when you come home. We moved because your Da read in the paper that most accidents happen within 20 miles of home. I won't be able to send you the address as the last family here took the numbers with them for their next house, so they wouldn't have to change their address.

Your loving Mother

PS I was going to send you ten euros, but I have already sealed the envelope.

Tiger Woods at a petrol station in Ireland bends over and some tees fall out of his pocket. "What are they?" asks the attendant. "They're called tees."

"But what are they for?" "They're to rest my balls on when I'm driving."

"Fookin' Jaysus, BMW t'inks of everything!"

[67]

An Irishman, an Englishman and a beautiful girl are riding together, the girl in the middle seat, in a train to Belfast. The train goes through a tunnel and it gets completely dark. Suddenly there is a kissing sound and then a slap. The train comes out of the tunnel. The woman and the Irishman are sitting there looking perplexed. The Englishman is bent over holding his face, which is red from a slap.

The Englishman is thinking, "Damn it, that Mick must have tried to kiss the girl, she thought it was me, and slapped me."

The girl is thinking, "That Englishman must have moved to kiss me and kissed the Irishman instead and got slapped."

The Irishman is thinking, "If this train goes through another tunnel, I could make another kissing sound and slap that damn Englishman again!"

There was a young lady called Etta
Who fancied herself in a sweata.
Three reasons she had,
Keeping warm was not bad,
But the other two reasons were betta.

A fellow walks into Murphy's bar, looking very down. The bartender pulls him a Guinness and says, "What's the matter? The fellow replies, "Well, I got these two horses and … well … I can't tell them apart. I don't know if I've fed them both or taken them both out for exercise. It's terrible, it is!" The bartender says, "Try shaving the tail of one of 'em." The man says, "I'll do that." A week or so later, he's back, down in the mouth. "The tail grew back. I vow I don't know what to do!" "Try shaving the mane, why don't you, and maybe that won't grow back." The fellow brightens and says he'll try that. He has a few drinks and leaves. A few months later, back he comes, looking distraught. "Well, it worked for awhile, but then the mane grew back and I'm at me wit's end." The bartender thinks the fellow is pretty dim and yells, "Jaysus, just measure the stupid horses. They can't be exactly the same!"
The fellow is back the next day, happy as can be. "It worked! It worked!" says he. "I measured the horses and the black one's two inches taller than the white one!"

A busload of politicians was driving down a country road near Galway, when suddenly a tire blew, the bus ran off the road and crashed into an old famer's barn. The old farmer got off his tractor and went to investigate the accident. Soon, he dug a large hole and buried the entire busload. Several days later, the local sheriff came out, saw the crashed bus, but no bodies, and asked the old farmer where all the politicians had gone.

"Sure, and I buried 'em."

The sheriff said, "Lordy, were they ALL dead?"

Said the old farmer, "Well, some of them said they weren't. But you know how them crooked politicians lie."

Mike Mayo went to visit his old mother for a cup of tea. He noticed that as she got the kettle and the cups and the strainer together, when she got to the medicine cabinet, she tiptoed very quietly.

"Mammy, why do you creep past that medicine cabinet?" Mike asked.

"Oh, I don't want to wake the sleeping pills."

A local Ballyvaughn man was taking a stroll on a Sunday, when he discovered a man in his sky-diving suit hanging from a tree branch.

"What happened to you?"

Said the sky diver: "I was skydiving and my parachute failed to open."

"You're not from around here, are you?"

"No, but what's that got to do with anything?"

"If you were a local man, you'd know that around here nothing opens on Sunday."

Finnegan checks into a Dublin hotel and has a porter accompany him to his room, carrying his bags.

As the door closes, Finnegan looks around and begins complaining.

"Oh, no, this room won't do. This isn't a double. Where's the en suite bathrooms and the French windows and the balcony? No this room is rubbish. I want it changed immediately."

"This isn't your room, Sir," says the porter. "It's the lift."

It was Sean's first day as a news reporter.
"Did you go and check out that story about
the woman who could sing soprano and alto
at the same time?" the editor asked.
"I did, Sir," said Sean. "But there wasn't a
story there. The woman just had two
heads."

Mary Maloney goes into a big department
store in Dublin and approaches the assistant
at the haberdashery counter.
"I'd like some fur gloves, please."
"Certainly, Madam," says the assistant.
"What fur?"
"Why, to keep my hands warm, of course."

Thaddeus bought his girlfriend her first
mobile phone for her birthday.
The next day, she was at a Boots when her
phone rang. It was her boyfriend.
"How do you like your new phone?"
"It's lovely, Thaddeus. But there's one thing
I just don't understand:
"How did you know I'd be here at Boots this
afternoon?"

"Mammy, I think you might be colour blind,"
said little Mary.
"Why, darlin'?"
"Because your rhubarb tart is made with
celery."

A girl from Kavan went for an interview and
the interviewer asked her age.
"Let me see," she said as she started
counting her fingers, then slipped off her
shoes and counted her toes, "I'm 19."
"Alright," said the interviewer. "And how tall
are you?"
The girl reached into her handbag, took out
a tape measure and announced, "I'm 5 feet
6 inches tall."
"And, d'ye know, I haven't got your name."
"Oh, I know that one! Just hang on a
minute, it'll come to me...now let's see...
'Happy birthday to me, happy birthday to
me, happy birthday dear...MAURA!"

"What's that mark on your face?" "A
birthmark."
"And how long have you had it, then?"

Many years ago, a baker's assistant called Richard the Pourer (his job was to pour the batter for the sausage rolls into the pan) noticed that he was running low on a spice he needed. He sent his apprentice to the spice shop.

Upon entering the shop, the apprentice realized he had forgotten the name of the spice.

All he could do was to tell the shopkeeper that it was for Richard the Pourer, for batter for wurst.

> A stunning young lady named Joyce
> Told us, "I have no R's in my voice.
> But I dance wock and woll
> Wear a wabbit-skin stole
> And dwive in a swanky Wolls Woyce."

Men are forgetful, whereas women remember everything. That's why men need instant replays in sports. They've already forgotten what happened.

There's a thin person inside every fat person. I ate mine.

Colleen was distraught when the Garda answered her call saying her car had been broken into.
"Look at this!" she wailed. "They took everything, everything! The radio, the cd player, the gear stick, the steering wheel, the dashboard, even!"
"Miss, please calm down," said the Garda. "And get out of the back seat."

The boss asked O'Brien, "Do you believe in life after death?"
"Yes, I do," said O'Brien.
"That's what I thought. Yesterday, after you left to go to your grandmother's funeral, she stopped by to see you."

One Sunday a four-year-old girl was acting up a bit during the 10:00 o'clock Mass. As her father carried her up the aisle, she cried: "Pray for me! Pray for me!"

CALLER: I'd like to speak with Seamus Fogerty.
ME: He's on vacation.
CALLER: I'll hold.

Fergus Houlihan went into the bank to see the Bank Director. When invited into the Director's office, he got straight to the point. "I was wondering, Sir...How do I stand to get a 500,000 euros loan?"
The Director studied Fergus for a few minutes and then said: "On your knees."

A judge rings up Donal Conroy, the lawyer. "How much would you charge me to answer three questions?"
"One thousand pounds," says Conroy.
"One thousand pounds!" exclaims the judge. "That's pretty expensive, isn't it?"
"To be sure, it is, Your Honour. And what might your last question be?"

"So how's the new diet going?" Liam asked Shaun when they met in the street.
"Oh, it's brilliant," said Shaun. "It's the whiskey diet."
"Whiskey diet? Never heard of it."
"I have whiskey for breakfast, whiskey for lunch, and whiskey for dinner."
"Is it working?"
"Well, last week I lost three days."

The Limerick Hotspurs Rover's goalkeeper let in 28 goals in one match. He trudged off the field feeling very dejected and with a nasty backache from all that bending over and picking the ball out of the back of the net.
He slunk into the changing room, where all his teammates completely ignored him.
He was so upset and distraught that he put his head in his hands to cry... and missed.

Ten-year-old Ciara was in her back garden filling in a rather large hole she had dug. Watching over the garden fence, her neighbor said, "What are you doing there darlin'?"
"I'm burying my pet goldfish, Rover."
"Oh dear," said the neighbor. "I'm sorry about Rover. But that's a big hole for such a little creature."
"I know," said Ciara. "But that's because he's inside your cat."

In Belfast City Hall, the Irish Philharmonic Orchestra was playing "Bermuda Rhapsody" and the triangle player disappeared.

Gerald was told by his landlord that he had two days to pay his overdue rent. Otherwise, he was out!

"Fine," said Gerald. "Can I have Easter Sunday and Christmas Day?"

A pair of tourists from England were traveling in Ireland for the very first time. The wife, in particular, loved the quaint architecture, the winding streets and the green green grass that happens when it rains a great deal.

She spied a rather strange looking fellow leaning up against a fence and said to him, "Please excuse me, I don't mean to be rude, but it's so traditional here in your village...Tell me, do you still have a village idiot these days?"

"Ah now, Missus, I'm afraid we have no village idiot at all, at all."

"Oh," she said, rather disappointed.

Then he added: "No, now we all take it in turns."

I just received a fax from our Irish branch. How do I know? It has a stamp on it.

the drink

THE BEST OF IRISH HUMOR

A Texan walks into a pub in Ireland and says to the crowd of drinkers. "I hear you Irish are a bunch of hard drinkers. I'll give $500 American to anybody in here who can drink 10 pints of Guinness back to back."
The room is quiet. Nobody answers and someone even gets up and leaves. The Texan shrugs and orders his own drink.
Thirty minutes later, the man who left shows up and says to the Texan, "Is your bet still good?"
"It sure is!" says the Texan, who asks the bartender to line up ten pints of Guinness. Immediately, the Irishman tears into all ten of the pint glasses, drinking them all, back to back.
The other pub patrons cheer as the Texan sits in amazement.
He gives the man his $500 and says, "If ya don't mind me askin', where did you go for that 30 minutes you weren't here?"
The Irishman replies:
"Oh...first I had to go to the pub down the street to see if I could do it."

At an Irish wedding reception someone yelled, "Would all the married men please stand next to the one person who has made your life really worth living!"
The bartender was almost crushed to death.

Higgins was staggering home with a pint of Irish Whisky in his back pocket, when he slipped and fell. He felt something wet running down his leg.
"Please God" he implored, "Let it be blood."

Pat and Mike have been drinking buddies for years.
One day Mike says to Pat,
"We've been friends for years, and if I should die before you, would you do me a favor? I want you to get the best bottle of Irish whiskey and pour it over my grave."
Pat replies,
"I'd be glad to do that for you old friend but would you mind if I passed it through my bladder first?"

An Irishman walks into a pub in England, orders three pints of Guinness and sits in the back of the room drinking a sip out of each one in turn. When he finishes them, he comes back to the bar and orders three more. The bartender says, "You know, a pint goes flat after I draw it. It would taste better if you bought one at a time."

The Irishman replies, "I have two brothers, one is in America and the other is in Canada. I'm here in Dublin. When we all left home, we promised that we'd drink this way to remember the days when we all drank together." The bartender admits that this is a very nice custom and leaves it there. The Irishman becomes a regular in the pub and always orders the same way.

One day he comes in and orders two pints. All the regulars notice and fall silent.

When he comes for the second round, the bartender says, "I want to offer my condolences on your loss".

The Irishman looks confused for a moment, then he laughs and says, "Oh no, everyone's okay, I've just quit drinking."

99-year-old Mother Superior of St. Bridget's was dying. The nuns gathered around her bed. They offered her a glass of warm milk and she took only one sip, then refused more. One of the nuns took the glass back to the kitchen and opened a bottle of Irish whisky, pouring a generous amount into the warm milk. Back at Mother Superior's bed, she held the glass to the old woman's lips. Mother drank a little, then a little more, and before they knew it she had emptied the entire glass. Then she lay back and seemed to fade a bit. "Please, Mother," one of the nuns said, "Give us some wisdom before you die."
Mother Superior suddenly sat up and said, "Whatever you do, don't sell that cow!"

The police car pulled over Father Murphy for speeding. "Have you been drinking, sir?"
"Only water, officer."
"But I smell wine."
Father Murphy looked down at an empty bottle on the floor, and said, "Good Lord, He's done it again!"

A drunk staggers into a Catholic Church, enters a confessional booth, sits down but says nothing.
The Priest coughs a few times to get his attention, but the drunk just sits there.
Finally, the priest pounds three times on the wall.
"Ain't no use knockin'" mumbles the drunk. "There's no toilet paper on this side, either."

One day an Englishman, Scotsman and an Irishman walked into a pub together. They each bought a pint of Guiness. Just as they were about to enjoy their drinks, three flies landed in each of their pints, and were stuck in the thick foam.
The Englishman pushed his beer away in disgust.
The Scotsman fished the fly out and continued to drink, as if nothing had happened.
The Irishman also picked the fly out of his drink, held it over the beer, and started yelling, "SPIT IT OUT! SPIT IT OUT! SPIT IT OUT!"

Drunkenness, for some strange reason, has a rich lexicon in Ireland. You can be ossified, fluthered, in the horrors, langers, locked, paralytic, plastered, scuttered, stocious, twisted and sizzled...to name just a few.

Seamus and Sean were out fishing in a boat, and the motor died. After two days of drifting miles from the shore, they found a bottle floating in the water. Pat rubbed the bottle and sure enough a Genie appeared.
"I will grant you one wish," said the Genie.
Without a thought, Sean said,
"I'd like it if the entire sea were Guinness."
The Genie said, "Your wish is my command," and poof! the sea turned into beer.
Seamus yelled at Sean, "You idiot!
"Now we'll have to pee in the boat!"

Flaherty staggered into the pub with a pig under one arm.
"Where in the world did you get him?" asked the bartender.
Said the pig, "Won him in a raffle!"

[86]

Keniry walks into a pub and orders a dozen
martinis. He removes the olives, placing
them in a jar, and drinks the martinis down.
When the jar is filled and the drink all gone,
he pays up and prepares to leave.
The barman stops him and says, "Excuse
me, but what was that all about?"
Keniry replies, "My wife sent me out for a jar
of olives."

If it's December and...
If you see a fat man who is jolly and cute,
Wearing a beard and a red flannel suit,
And if he is chuckling and laughing away,
While flying around in a miniature sleigh,
With eight tiny reindeer to pull him along...
Then let's face it, your eggnog's too strong!

Siobahn followed her husband to the pub.
"How can you come here all the time," she
asked, after taking a sip of his Guinness
Stout. "and drink this terrible stuff?"
"There now!" he cried. "And you always
thought I was out enjoying meself!"

[87]

Sean is a drunk. A priest meets him one day and tells him that, if he continues drinking like that he will get smaller and smaller and turn into a mouse.

Sean goes home and tells his wife, "If you notice me getting smaller and smaller, please kill the cat."

An Irishman finds an old lamp and, when rubbing it clean, out pops a Genie.

"Master, you have released me from the lamp," says the Genie, "and you therefore are entitled to three wishes."

Irishman scratches his head, then says, "All right, then, a bottle of Guinness that never gets empty."

"Granted," says the Genie and a large bottle of Guinness appears. Irishman stays drunk for weeks. One day he wakes up and remembers that he has two more wishes. He rubs the lamp again and the Genie appears as before. "You have two more wishes, Master."

"I'd like two more of those magic Guinness bottles."

"I've bad news for you, Brenda Malloy," said
Flynn, coming into the Malloy's kitchen.
"It's your husband."
"Where is he?"'
"There was an accident down at the
brewery. Seamus fell into a vat of Guinness
Stout and drowned."
"Oh, dear Jesus! Seamus is dead! But you
must tell me true, Flynn. Did he at least go
quickly?"
"Well...no, Brenda, no."
"Saints preserve us, no?"
"Fact is...he got out three times to pee."

Mulrooney goes to Switzerland to climb the
Matterhorn.
He hires a guide, and they're caught in an
avalanche.
Five hours later, a St. Bernard reaches them
with a small barrel of brandy under his chin.
"Hooray!" shouts the guide. "Here comes
man's best friend!"
"Indeed," says Mulrooney. "And look at the
size of the dog that's bringing it!"

A man stumbles up to the only other patron in a bar and asks could he buy him a drink.
"Why, certainly," comes the reply.
The first man then asks, "Where are you from?"
"I'm from Ireland."
"You don't say!" cries the first man. "I'm from Ireland, too! Let's have another round to Ireland."
Of course," the other agrees. They lift their glasses, and the first man says, "Where in Ireland?"
"County Cork."
"You don't say! Me, too, I'm from County Cork. Let's have another drink to County Cork!"
"So what school did you attend?" says the first.
"St. Mary's."
"St. Mary's! And might you have graduated in'62?" "I did!"
"This is unbelievable!" they say together.
About this time, a regular comes into the bar. "What's up?" he asks the barman.
"Not much. The Harrigan twins are drunk again."

What's an Irish mixed grill? Mashed potato, roast potato, boiled potato, chips, and a case of Guinness.

The local District Judge had given the defendant a lecture on the evils of drink.
But since this was the first offense, the case was dismissed on payment of twenty euros cost.
"Now don't let me ever see your face again," the judge said.
"I'm afraid I can't promise that, sir," said the man.
"And why not?"
"Because I'm the barman at your regular pub."

The doctor was puzzled.
"I'm sorry," he said, "But I just can't diagnose your trouble, O'Malley.
"I think it must be drink."
"Oh, that's all right," said O'Malley.
"I'll come back after you sober up."

Pat walks into the pub, a sack over his shoulder. His mate, Tim, who's already had a few too many says, "What's in the sack?" "Some ducks," says Pat. "If you can guess how many, I'll give you both of them." Quickly, Tim says, "Three."

Abbey Ale's what we brew here, we
Trappists.
(We're in Belgium, for all of you mappists.)
Strong and rich, full in body,
As sweet as a Toddy
I'm glad that we're brewers, not frappists.

Every man has beliefs he holds dear,
Where his faith is unshakably clear.
My belief is devout,
With no shadow of doubt;
I believe that I'll order more beer!

When you're down 'cause a confidant fails
you
Or your bitterest enemy nails you.
Draw a blackjack of bitter
And don't be a quitter!
(I'm told that it's good for what ails you!)

[92]

A bibulous fellow named Gooch
As he thought he drank far too much hooch
Decided to try
To cut down on it by
Drinking no more than what he could
mooch.

A brewery worker named Fred
Had a barrel fall onto his head.
"Weren't you hurt?" I did ask,
"Being hit by that cask?"
"I was lucky – 'twas light ale," he said.

"A beer? A big one or small?
The tender asked me from his stall.
"Or medium? Which size?
Choose well and choose wise."
"Oh, sod!" says I. "I'll have them all!"

There was a young girl, Mary Spratt,
At work one day, fell in a vat.
Before she was dragged out
She had drunk so much stout
That her thin parts had all turned to fat.

One day Riley, man of good cheer
Asked Descartes if he'd care for a beer.
To his surprise what he got
Was a low, "I think not."
As he watched Descartes go disappear.

'Tis a terrible thing to be dead
Or to sleep all alone in a bed,
But next to it, lad,
There is nothing so sad
As a beer which is minus a head.

On Patty's Day, there's Sean O'Malley
Guzzling Guinness alone in an alley.
How much can he drink
I really can't think,
And O'Malley, he never keeps talley.

The fire engine sped up the street, all bells clanging, just as Mick staggered out of the pub. He promptly chased after the fleeing truck but soon collapsed, exhausted.
"All right then!" he shouted from the pavement. "You can keep yer bloody ice cream!"

Michael McCool came home drunk every night toward ten and the missus, now, was never too happy about it, either.

So one night she hides herself in the cemetery, on Michael's path home, and as poor Mike comes staggering by, she jumps up in a red devil costume screaming, "Michael John Anthony McCool, sure and if you don't give up your drinkin', it's to Hell I'm going to take you and that's certain!"

Undaunted, Mikie staggers back and demands, "Who the hell ARE you??"

"I'm the divil, ya damned old fool!"

To which McCool remarks,

"Damned glad to meet you, sir.

"I'm married to your sister!"

A Garda pulls up two drunks in Galway and says to the first, "Name and address, please."

"I'm Paddy O'Day of no fixed address."

The cop turns to the second drunk and repeats the question.

"I'm Seamus O'Toole and I live in the flat above Paddy."

"All that money you had and now you're skint," says O'Kane to Harrigan. "What happened to it all?"
"Most of it I spent on women and drink," says Harrigan. "The rest I just squandered."

A golf club walks into the pub and asks the barman for a pint. The barman says no.
"Why not?"
"Because you'll be driving later."

George Bernard Shaw said: "Alcohol is a very necessary article. It enables Parliament to do things at eleven at night that no sane person would do at eleven in the morning."

O'Hara phoned the police to report that thieves had been in his car. "They've stolen the dashboard, the steering wheel, the radio, even the brake!"
Three minutes later, he called back again.
"Never mind," he said with a hiccup. "I got in the back seat by mistake."

After the Britain Beer Festival in London, all the brewery presidents decided to go out for a beer. The president of Corona says, "Senor, I would like the world's best beer, a Corona." The barman dusts off a bottle and hands it to him.
The guy from Budweiser says, "I'd like the King of Beers, Budweiser." The barman gives him one.
The president of Coors says, "I'd like the only beer made with Rocky Mountain spring water. Give me a Coors and make it cold." He gets it.
The president of Guinness sits down and says, "I'll have a Coke."
The bartender is taken aback but pours him a Coke.
The other brewery presidents look over at him and one of them says, "Why aren't you having a Guinness?"
He smiles and replies, "Well, I figured if you guys aren't drinking beer, neither would I."

How to dance the Irish jig.
1. Drink plenty of beer. 2. Lock the toilets.

A rather ugly girl came into Donegan's Pub the other night and asked me what did reincarnation mean?
"It means that after you die, you come back again, but as something else," says I.
"When I come back, I want to be a dog," she tells me.
"Missy," says I, "you're not listenin' to me at all, are ya?"

A grasshopper walks into a pub and the bartender says, "Ye know, we got a drink named after you!" The grasshopper looks surprised. "Begorrah," he says. "There's a drink named Kevin?"

A fellow in the pub is ordering three or four shots of whisky at a time and throwing them back as fast as he can.
The bartender says, "Why would you be drinking so fast, man?"
"You'd be drinking fast too, if you had what I had." "And what might you be having?"
"No money."

GREAT QUOTES FROM GREAT DRINKERS

24 hours in a day ... 24 bottles of beer in a case. Coincidence? I think not.
> –Steven Wright

Always do sober what you said you'd do drunk. That'll teach you to keep your mouth shut.   -Ernest Hemingway

Here's to alcohol, the rose-colored glasses of life.   -F. Scott Fitzgerals

In wine there is wisdom, in beer there is freedom, in water there is bacteria.
> -Benj. Franklin

I like to have a martini,
Two at the very most.
After three I'm under the table,
After four I'm under my host.
> –Dorothy Parker

I cook with wine. Sometimes I even add it to the food.   -W. C. Fields

A man walks into a pub, sits down, and orders a drink.
"Sure, and that's a nice shirt!" comes out of nowhere. He looks all around to see who might have said it but no one looks at him.
"Sure, and you're lookin' real good tonight!"
Now the man calls to the barkeep and says, "Do you keep talkin' to me?"
"It's not me, it's the complimentary nuts."

It was a slow night at Cassidy's pub when the stranger came in. He sat down at the bar, but ordered nothing.
"Would you like a beer?" asked the bartender. "Just Coke. I don't drink. I tried it once but didn't like it."
"Would you like a cigarette?"
"No, thanks, I don't smoke. Tried it once, didn't like it."
"Well, then, they're lookin' for someone to shoot pool over there."
"I tried that once. Didn't like it. I wouldn't be here, but my son asked me to meet him."
The barman said,
"Your only child, I'm thinkin'?"

Sean and Seamus, both of them drunk, are staggering home. Sean says, "What a beau'ful night. Just look at that moon!" Seamus stops and looks up at the sky. "Tha's not the moon, tha's the sun!" "Moon!" "Sun!" Then they see another drunk weaving his way toward them. They stop him. "Could you be tellin' us what that thing is, up in the sky? Is it the moon or is it the sun, sor?" The third man looks up to examine the sky, then says, "Sure and I'm sorry, but I don't live around here."

A man at the local pub said to a woman next to him, "This is a special day. I'm celebrating." "What a coincidence," said she. "I'm celebrating meself. What happened for you?" "I'm a chicken farmer and for years my hens were infertile, but not now. You?" "What a coincidence. For years I couldn't get pregnant, but I am now. How did you manage to do it?" "Switched cocks," said the chicken farmer. "What a coincidence."

A man walks into a pub and orders a pint.
The bartender serves him and says, "That'll
be four Euros."
The customer pulls out a twenty Euro note
and hands it to the bartender.
"Sorry, sor, but I cannot accept that."
The man pulls out a ten Euro note but that's
not acceptable, either.
"Why won't you take my money?" he asks
The bartender points to a sign at the front of
the pub, saying SINGLES BAR.

The manager of a liquor store gets a phone
call at 8:00 PM.
"What time do you open tomorrow?" asks
the caller. "At 9:00."
The phone rings at midnight. "What time
d'ya open inna mornin'?" "I told you: at 9
o'clock."
Just before closing, the phone rings again.
It's the same man, his voice very slurred.
"Wa' time...hic ... yez open ...?"
"I've told you and told you. Why do you
want to know?"
""I'm inna hurry 'cause I got locked in your
storeroom las' night."

LIMERICKS FOR BEER LOVERS

It wasn't a real hard decision
That with millimeter precision
I removed the crown
And poured the beer down
My beer belly collection addition.

I knew I would be ad libbin'.
My buddies all thought I was kiddin'.
Used some old malt I could find,
And a lot of old hops off the vine;
And, you know, I won a blue ribbon!

Said a guy who liked to drink beer,
"To me it is perfectly clear:
The more suds you drink,
The better you think!"
And promptly fell flat on his rear.

There was a fat fella called Buddha
Who weighed thirty stone, though he coulda
Laid off the lard
And ale by the yard,
As a proper divine being shoulda.

Oh my lord, my face is so pale
Like zero on a one-to-ten scale
All sick and obscure.
Could there be any cure?
Of course! A cold bottle of ale!

A jolly old tipple named Charlie
Engaged, in a pub, in a parley.
With a wink, said, "I think
That your drink's turning pink:
A sign of inferior barley.

As from Monday, the second of June,
When the clock in my bedroom says noon,
I will stop drinking beer
For the rest of the year
(Or until I go near a saloon.)

Oh, beer, thou drink of the gods,
Have pity on all us poor sods.
Like bees to a flower
Give us the power
In quantities best known as "lots."

I went to the worst of pubs hoping to get
killed, but I only got drunk again.

[104]

Harrigan has had a drop too much to drink and his car is weaving from one side of the road to the other. The Garda pulls him over. "I see you've had a few drinks too many this night," he says to Harrigan. "I did have a bit," says Harrigan. "Well," says the Guarda, "did you know that three streets back, your wife fell out of the car?" "Oh, thank God!" says Harrigan. "For a minute there, I thought I'd gone deaf!"

Murphy approached Mulligan's bar. Outside the entrance he was accosted by a nun "I'm Sister Mary Benedict," she said in a stern voice, "and I cannot believe a fine man such as yourself is going to go into this den of iniquity!" "Hang on there, Sister. How can you condemn someone out of hand like that. What do you know of the drink, since you've never had a taste?"
"I shouldn't judge. Why don't you get me a large gin and have them put it in a cup." Murphy agreed and went in to get it.
"My God," said the barkeep. "Is that nun still outside?"

Donegan and his wife are awakened at 3 o'clock in the morning by a loud pounding on their front door. Donegan gets up and opens the door to a drunken stranger, who is standing in a pouring rain, asking for a push.

"Not on yer life," says Donegan. He slams the door and returns to bed.

"Who was that?" asks his wife.

"Oh, just some drunk, asking for a push."

"And you didn't help him? Well, for shame, Daniel Donegan! Don't you remember last month when you broke down? Two nice men helped us, remember? And it was pretty late, and it was raining. Weren't you grateful then? You should go out and help the poor fella."

Donegan has to agree. He gets himself dressed, finds his Wellies and his rain gear and slogs out into the night.

Into the dark, he calls out: "Still there?"

"Yes, for sure!"

"And you still need a push?"

"Yes, indeed I do."

"Where are you?'

"Over here, on the swing!"

Seven Signs You May Be Drinking Too Much

1. You lose arguments with inanimate objects.

2. Your job interferes with your drinking.

3. You believe that a drinking problem is having two hands and just one mouth.

4. The world comes into focus when you use just one eye.

5. Your car mysteriously moves every time you leave the pub.

6. You don't remember the words to a song to which you gladly play air guitar.

7. You have to hang onto the floor to keep from falling off the planet.

A lady came up to me one day and said, "Sir, you are drunk!"
To which I replied, "I am drunk today and tomorrow I shall be sober. But you will still be ugly."   -Winston Churchill

AN INTERVIEW ABOUT DRINKING

Lady Reporter: Do you drink?
Murphy: Yes.

Lady Reporter: How much a day?
Murphy: Around half a bottle of whisky.

Lady Reporter: How much does whisky cost?
Murphy: I'd say roughly thirty Euros.

Lady Reporter: How long have you been drinking like that?
Murphy: Thirty years, more or less.

Lady Reporter: That means you've spent around E150,000 on booze.
Murphy: Begorrah, have I indeed?

Lady Reporter: If you didn't drink, you could have bought a Ferrari.
Murphy: (thinks) Tell me, do YOU drink?

Lady Reporter: No, I do not.
Murphy: So where is your Ferrari?

An Irishman, an Englishman and a Scot were sitting in a bar in Sydney, Australia. The view was great, the beer excellent, and the food exceptional.

"But," said the Scot, "I still prefer the pubs back home. Why, in Glasgow, in McTavish's Bar, the landlord always buys the fifth drink for you."

"Well," countered the Englishman, "At my local, the Red Lion, the barman there will buy your third drink after you have two."

"Ha, that's nothin'," says the Irishman. "Back home in Dublin, there's Ryan's Pub. Now the moment you set foot in the place they'll buy you a drink, then another ... all the drink you like. Then, when you've had enough, they'll take you upstairs and see that you get laid. And all of this is on the house, mind."

The other two men were scornful. "Did this actually happen to you?" says the Scot.

"Well, not meself personally, no," admitted the Irishman.

 "But it happened all the time to me sister Bridey."

The tired long-distance truck driver goes into the pub and says to the bartender, "I'd like a shot of gin."
The bartender is bored and decides to have a bit of fun.
"Okay, but what kind of gin would you be wanting?"
"There's only one kind of gin, man!"
"Not really. You've got hydrogen, oxygen and nitrogen."
The trucker says, "I see. Well, did you know there are three kinds of turds?"
The bartender says: "Three kinds of turds?"
"Well," says the trucker, "we've got mustard, and we've got custard and now we've got you, you big turd. Now give me my shot of gin!"

SYMPTOM: Floor blurred.
FAULT: You are looking through the bottom of an empty glass.
ACTION: Get someone to buy you a beer.

SYMPTOM: Room unusually dark.
FAULT: Bar has closed.
ACTION: Confirm home address.

O'Banion wakes up in his bed at home with a horrible hangover. He forces his eyes open and immediately sees a couple of aspirins and a glass of water on the side table. He gets up and sees clothes for the day, all cleaned and pressed. The room is in perfect order, spotless, clean. And so is the rest of the house. He takes the aspirin and notices a note on the kitchen table. "Dear, breakfast is on the stove. Left early to go shopping. Love you. Agnes."

Sure enough, there is a hot breakfast and the morning paper. His son is at the table. O'Banion says, "Matthew, what's happened last night?"

"Well, you came home after 3 in the morning, drunk and delirious. You broke some furniture, puked in the hallway and gave yourself a black eye hitting a door."

O'Banion is well and truly confused. "So why is everything in order, all neat and clean and breakfast waiting for me?"

"Oh, that! Ma dragged you to the bedroom, and when she tried to take your pants off, you yelled, "Lady, leave me alone, I'm a married man!"

[111]

There once was a guy name of Mudd
Who really liked to drink Bud.
He drank about ten
With his porcelain friend,
And then said goodnight with a thud.

Some merry old monks of Manuller
Found life was becoming much duller.
They brewed a fine ale
In a massive big pail,
And they found their lives were much fuller.

His wife almost bankrupted Meer
With daily requests for more beer.
And when ready to die
She so feared to be dry
She insisted a keg be nigh her here.

There once was a man from Dowd Flat
Who fell in a brewery vat.
He drank it all dry
Without getting high,
And asked where the men's room was at.

Paddy, Murphy, and O'Shea went into the pub and ordered this way:

Murphy: I'll have a B and C.
Bartender: What's a B and C?
Murphy: Bourbon and Coke.
O'Shea: And I'll have a G and T.
Bartender: What's a G and T?
O'Shea: Gin and tonic.
Paddy: I'll have a 15.
Bartender: What's a 15?
Paddy: 7 and 7.

SYMPTON: Beer tasteless, front of shirt is wet.
FAULT: Mouth not open or glass applied to wrong part of face.
ACTION: Retire to restroom, practice in the mirror.

SYMPTOM: Feet cold and wet.
FAULT: Glass held at incorrect angle.
ACTION: Rotate glass so that open end points toward the ceiling.

After a heavy night at the pub, Brian decided to sleep it off at a local hotel. He approached the reception desk, took care of the formalities, and headed off to his suite. Several minutes later, there he was, staggering back to the desk, demanding that his room be changed.

"But sir," said the clerk, "you have the best room in the hotel!'

Brian insisted, vociferously.

"Very well, sir, I'll change you from 525 to 505. Would you mind telling me why you don't like 525?"

"Well, for one thing," said Brian. "It's on fire."

What's an Irishman's martini?
An olive in a glass of beer.

Flannery walks into a pub and asks the bartender if he'll give him a free Guiness for an amazing trick. The bartender agrees. So Flannery pulls out a hamster from his jacket and the little animal begins to sing and dance on the bar.

"That IS amazing," says the bartender.

Flannery says, "If I show you something even more amazing than that, will you give me another free beer?"

The answer is yes.

Flannery pulls out a toy piano and a frog. The hamster plays the piano while the frog sings and dances on the bar.

The barman, completely wowed, gives him another beer.

A man down the bar who's been watching all of this offers to buy the frog for 100 pounds.

"Shure," says Flannery. "And here he is!"

When the purchaser leaves, the barman says, "Are you after being crazy? You could make a fortune offa that frog and you let him go for so little money?"

"Can you keep a secret?" says Flannery. "That frog is a fraud. The hamster's a ventriloquist."

DRUNK: Bartender! My beer is flat and tasteless!
BARTENDER: I'll fix that, sir.
DRUNK: A different beer?
BARTENDER: No, your glass is empty.

A drunk staggers out of his local pub. The first person he sees, he stops, saying, "I'm Jesus Christ." "No you're not."
He walks up to another pedestrian and says, "I'm Jesus Christ." "That's bloody nonsense." Says the drunk, "If you'll just come with me, I'll prove it."
So the three of them walk into the pub and the barman says, "Jesus Christ, you again?"

Into a bar in Galway walked an Irishman, an Italian, a Swiss, a German, a Frenchman, an American, an Englishman, a Zulu, a Cambodian, an Israeli, an Egyptian, a Dutchman, a Serb, a Russian, an Indian and a Czech.
The barman calls out, "I'm sorry, but I can't let you in without a Thai."

An older man, driving rather badly, is stopped by the Garda around 1:00 AM. And where might he be going this time of night? "I'm going to a lecture about the evils of alcohol." And who might be giving such a lecture so late at night? asks the Garda.
The man replies: "Me wife."

Practice makes perfect
There's many do think.
But a man's not too perfect
When he's practiced at drink.

A man takes a drink; the drink takes a
drink; the drink takes the man.

Murphy, Collins, and Vella are drinking in the
local pub when a very drunk man comes
weaving in. He points at Collins, shouting,
"Your Mum's the best shag in town!"
Everyone at the bar expects a fight but
Collins ignores him and the drunk wanders
off to the other end of the bar, where he
puts his nose in a pint of Guinness.
After ten minutes, he's back, yelling to
Collins, "I just screwed your mum and it was
grand!" Again, he is ignored and again he
goes back to the other end of the bar.
Ten minutes go by and he's back again,
shouting: "Your mum said it was the best
thing since sliced bread!"
Finally Collins talks back. "Go home, Da,"
he says. "You're pissed!"

[117]

Brian O'Hara drives a double-decker bus in Dublin. One day a very drunk Tim Fogarty climbed aboard. There's a law in Dublin says you cannot have a drunken person aboard a city bus; but Brian was feeling good and he thought he'd let this one by. But Fogarty, in the way of drunks everywhere, began to talk a blue streak. As the other passengers began to notice, Brian suggested to Fogarty that he go upstairs. "You'll get some fresh air up there and there's a grand view," he said. Fogarty agreed.

He was back ten minutes later. "It was nice up there," he said, "but much too dangerous."

"Dangerous how?" asked Brian.

"No driver up there."

When we drink, we get drunk. When we get drunk, we fall asleep. When we fall asleep, we commit no sin. When we commit no sin, we go to heaven.

Soooo, let's all get drunk and go to heaven!

-Brian O'Rourke

Jim O'Dowd was drinking all the weekend, so he was clearly inebriated when he walked into Doyle's bar. He sat down and demanded a drink.

The bartender said, "Get out. I don't serve drunks here."

Jim acknowledged that fact and staggered out the front door. A few minutes later, he came in through the back door, sat at the bar, banged his first and demanded a drink.

"Bejesus! I just told you to get out, didn't I? Now LEAVE!"

Jim got off his stool and stumbled out the back door, only to appear once more through the side door. Once again, he banged on the bar and hollered for a drink.

The bartender, now mad, glared at Jim O'Dowd and yelled, "I TOLD YOU, NO DRUNKS ALLOWED!"

Jim looked up and the bartender and said, "How many bars do you work at, anyway?"

Two drunks get on a city bus. "Can you take me to Duncan street?" asks one.

"No."

"But can you take <u>me</u>?" asks the second.

Recently a routine police patrol parked outside a local pub in Dublin. Late in the evening, the officer noticed a man leaving the bar so drunk he could barely walk. He stumbled around the car park, trying his car key on five vehicles and finally found his car and fell into it. He was there a few minutes as a number of other cars left, unable to start his vehicle. Finally he started the car, switched the wipers on and off instead of the lights, tooted the horn and at last switched on the lights. He drove forward, stopped, reversed, stopped, and then he stalled out. The police officer waited patiently until at last, the car pulled out of the car park, indicated a left turn and turned right and started down the road.

Now the police car pulled out, turned on his flashing lights, pulled the man over and gave him a breathalyzer test. To his amazement, the test showed no presence of alcohol.

"I'm taking you in," he said. "This analyzer must be broken."

"I doubt it," said the man. "Tonight I'm the Designated Decoy."

Ho! Ho! Ho! To the bottle I go
To heal my heart and drown my woe
Rain may fall, and wind may blow
And many miles be still to go
But under a tall tree will I lie
And let the clouds go sailing by.
                              -J.R.R. Tolkien

A tippler who swore he'd stopped drinking
Passed a pub and, hearing glass clinking,
             Upended a flagon,
             Fell off of the wagon,
And into the gutter dropped, stinking.

A vision of loveliness fair,
I'm quite certain I see over there.
             Is it Molly or Carole?
             Oh, no, it's a barrel
Of Old Thumper Ale, I declare.

There once was a girl named Anhauser
Who said that no man could surprise her.
             But Pabst took a chance,
             Found the Schlitz in her pants,
And now she is sadder Budweiser.

So you hate your job?
 Why didn't you say so? There's a support group for that.
It's called EVERYBODY, and they meet at the bar.
                                        -Drew Carey

I went out with a guy once who told me I didn't need to drink to be more fun to be around. I told him, I'm drinking so YOU'RE more fun to be around.
                          -Chelsea Handler

I thought such awful thoughts that I cannot even say them out loud because they would make Jesus want to drink gin straight out of the cat dish.   -Anne Lamott

Laugh whenever you can. Keeps you from killing yourself when things are bad.
That and vodka.   -Jim Butcher

I've reached the age where Happy Hour is a nap.

Can I wear high heels in Australia?
You're an Irish politician, right?

An Irish youth proves his manhood by getting stuck in a pint, in a woman, and in a fish—in that order.

It's the first drop that destroys you; there's no harm at all in the last.

The devil invented Scotch whiskey to make the Irish poor.

The truth comes out when the spirit goes in.

Drink is the curse of the land.
It makes you fight with your neighbor. It makes you shoot at your landlord...
and it makes you miss him.

Before you call for one for the road, be sure you know the road.

Flynn staggered home very late after another evening of drinking. He took off his shoes to avoid waking his wife Maura.
He tiptoed to the stairs but misjudged the bottom step. As he grabbed the banister, his body swung around and he landed heavily on his rear. A whiskey bottle in each back pocket broke. Managing not to yell, Flynn got up, pulled down his pans and looked in the hall mirror to see that his butt was cut and bleeding. He quietly found a box of Band-Aids and began to apply them as best he could on every place where he could see blood. He then hid the almost-empty Band-Aid box and stumbled and shuffled his way up the stairs and into bed.
In the morning, Flynn woke up with searing pain in both his head and his rear end; and with Maura staring at him. "You were drunk again last night, weren't you?" she said.
Flynn said, "Why would you say such a mean thing?"
"Well, it could be the open front door or the broken glass on the stairs, or the trail of blood. But mostly, it's all those Band-Aids stuck on the hall mirror."

There was an old drunk called Hieronymus,
Who joined Alcoholics Anonymus;
But with liver disease,
The shakes and D. T's
The prognostication is ominous. −R. Rubin

There was a young girl whose frigidity
Approached cataleptic rigidity,
'Til you gave her a drink,
When she quickly would sink
In a state of complaisant liquidity.

On the chest of a barmaid in Sale
Were tattooed the prices of ale,
And on her behind
For the sake of the blind
Was the same information in Braille.

The handsome young barkeep at Sweeney's
Is famed for his ale and free wienies.
But I thought him uncouth
To gulp gin and vermouth,
Chill the glasses, and piddle Martinis.

In considering things gastronomic
Cakes and ale are not quite economic.
Though maybe we oughter
Stick to plain bread and water,
It's gin makes a tonic a tonic.

There was an old man in a trunk
Who inquired of his wife, "Am I drunk?"
She replied with regret,
"I'm afraid so, my pet."
And he answered, "It's just as I thunk."

There was a young girl of Donmeer
Whose reflex reactions were queer.
Her escort said, "Mabel,
Get up off the table."
"That money is there for the beer."

An amoeba named Sam and his brother
Were having a drink with each other.
In the midst of their quaffing,
They split themselves laughing
And each of them now if a mother.

Before performing a christening in Sligo,
Father Duffy approached Seamus and said
to him solemnly: "Baptism is a serious step.
Are ye prepared for it?"
"I think I am, Father," Seamus replied. "My
wife has made a big buffet spread and Mrs.
Sullivan has baked biscuits and cakes for all
our guests."
"That's not what I meant," said the priest.
"I mean, are you prepared spiritually?"
"To be sure, I am," Seamus replied. "I've
got a keg of beer and a case of whiskey."

Two Limerickmen were in a bar having a
beer and chatting.
"If you had a choice," said the one, "and
could talk to anyone, living or dead, who
would it be?"
"The living one, for sure," said the other.

I've thought and I've thank and I've thunk
I've sought, then I sank, now I'm sunk.
Thirst I could not bear;
I'm now worse for wear.
For the drought, well I drank, now I'm
drunk.

[127]

There once was a brewer named Dale
Who only made fine amber ale.
He then had a daughter
Whom he caught drinking porter
So he kicked her right out on her tail.

Oh beer! I love how you taste
I drink with far too much haste
I'd not go a day without
A lager or stout
If not for the girth of my waist.

Add barley and hops to a kettle
And quality water. Don't settle!
On top, yeast's fermenting
(with adequate venting)
And brewing an ale of fine fettle.

There was a young lady of Ryde
Who ate some green apples and died.
The apples fermented
Inside the lamented
And made cider inside her inside.

[128]

Took seconds before 'twas okay.
From A to Z, all the way.
Feeling fresh and alright,
Shining bright as a light.
Once again beer has saved us the day.

There once was a drunken old boffin
Who remarked, in a fine fit of coughin'
"It isn't the cough
That carries you off,
But the coffin they carries you off in."

SYMPTOM: your singing sounds distorted.
FAULT: The beer is too weak.
ACTION: Have more beer until your voice improves.

SYMPTOM: Don't remember the words to the song.
FAULT: Not the beer; it's just right.
ACTION: Play air guitar.

Nobody goes to that pub anymore; it's too crowded.

[129]

Finegan had died and his wife Brigit invited everyone back to the house for the wake. Finegan's brother was the first one into the house. He saw that the front room was filled with crates of stout and cider, lager, whiskey, beer, and wine. On the table near the mountain of drink was a plate with two slices of bread on it.

Finegan's brother said, "Brigit, what's all the bread for?"

A drunk walks into a pub and says to the barman, "Buy everyone in the house a drink, give yourself one, and give me the bill." The bill is 54 euros. The man says, "I haven't got that much." The barman roughs him up a bit and throws him into the street. The very next day, the same drunk comes in and gives the same order: drinks for the house, one for the barman and the bill goes to the drunk.

The barman thinks, Can this fella really try to pull the same trick twice? No, probably not; he wouldn't dare.

But he does. When he is presented with the total of 67 euros, he says, "I haven't got it."

The barman really gives it to him this time, slaps him around, tells him to never show his face again in this pub, and throws him into the street.

And yet, the next day, there he is again, saying, "Barman, a drink for everyone in the house and give the bill to me."

Sarcastically: "What! No drink for me this time?"

Says the drunk: "You! Never again! You get too violent when you drink!"

Brian Boyle walks into his local with a giraffe and they sit down at adjoining stools. Brian says to the barman: "Two pints, please." He and the giraffe each drink one and then Brian asks for two more, which they both drink; and then two more and two more. After about 17 pints each, the giraffe begins to wobble on his stool. Finally, the animal just passes out and falls backwards onto the floor. Brian looks at the giraffe, pays their bill, and begins to walk out of the door. "Oi! You can't just leave that lyin' here!" yells the barman. Brian says, "That's not a lion, that's a giraffe," and walks on out.

Mike, drunk as usual, staggered into a bar and after staring at the only woman in the place for a while, walked up to her and gave her a kiss. She smacked him, hard. Mike apologized, saying, "I'm sorry, you look so much like my wife..."
"You're nothin' but a worthless, eejit of a drunk, you wretched excuse for a man!"
"Funny," Mike muttered, "You sound just like her, too."

Donncha, the barman, says to the stranger at his bar, "What'll it be?"
In a strong Kerry accent, the fellow says, "I'll have a scotch, please."
"That'll be 7 euros."
"What do you mean, man? I don't owe you a thing for this drink."
Donal, a lawyer sitting at the bar, says to Donncha: "He's got you there, y'know. In the original offer, which constitutes a binding contract upon acceptance, there was no stipulation of remuneration."
Donncha is unimpressed with the lawyerese and says to the Kerryman, "Alright, you got

me for a drink. But don't let me catch you comin' in here again."

The next day, the Kerryman is back.

Donncha glowers. "What the heck are you doin' back here again? You got some nerve!"

Kerryman smiles and says, "I don't know what you're talkin' about. I've never been here before in me life."

Donncha looks closely at him and mutters: "It's uncanny. You must have a double."

"Why thank you, barman, make it a scotch."

Dylan Thomas said: an alcoholic is someone you like who drinks as much as you do.

Maureen was fast asleep in bed when her husband Cormac crashed through the front door, waking her up.

He staggered through the hallway and struggled to get up the stairs.

"What are you doing?" shouted Maureen.

"I'm tryin' to get this gallon of beer up the stairs!"

"Leave it down there, Cormac!"

"I can't," he shouted. "I've drunk it!"

From a County Cork newspaper:
Reilly's Bar: Due to the sad death of
Shamus, the bar to all intents and purposes,
will remain closed during our grief, but so as
not to inconvenience our esteemed
customers, the door will remain ajar. 'Tis
what Shamus wanted. Thank you.

An Irish politician was asked for his position
on drinking. "If you mean the demon drink
that poisons the mind, pollutes the body,
desecrates family life, and inflames sinners,
then I'm totally and thoroughly against it.
"But if you mean the elixir of Christmas
cheer, the shield against winter chill, the
taxable potion that puts needed funds into
public coffers to comfort little crippled
children and the needy elderly, then I'm for
it. This is my position and I will not
compromise."

On the counter it stood—the glass
With a shiny colour like brass.
It was beer indeed
And I grabbed it in greed.
Such a chance I could not let pass by.

Doctor O'Hogan always stopped at his local after office hours, for a hazelnut daiquiri, a drink created for him by the barman, Dermot. One day Dermot ran out of hazelnut flavouring and substituted hickory nuts.
The doctor took one sip and said, "This isn't a hazelnut daiquiri, Dermot!"
"No, I'm sorry," said Dermot. "It's a hickory daiquiri, Doc."

Two drunks were arguing in a bar in Dublin.
First drunk: God bless Israel!
Second drunk: Screw Israel!
First drunk: God bless Netanyahu!
Second drunk: Screw Bibi!
First drunk: Are you Jewish?
Second drunk: No. I'm Irish.
First drunk: Then screw Ella Fitzgerald!

A man walked into a bar with an alligator under his arm.
He asked the barman, "Do you serve lawyers here?"
"Yes, of course."
"Well, then, I'll have a whisky and a lawyer for my alligator."

I'm a social drinker. Every time someone says, "I think I'll have a drink," I say, "And social I."

On the menu of a Galway restaurant: OUR WINES LEAVE YOU NOTHING TO HOPE FOR

THE BEER PRAYER

Our lager, which art in barrels,
Hallowed be thy drink.
Thy will be drunk
(I will be drunk)
At home as at three seasons.

Give us this day our foamy head
And forgive us our spillage
As we forgive those who spill against us.
And lead us not into incarceration
But deliver us from hangovers
For thine is the beer
The bitter and the lager
Forever and ever,
Barmen.

[136]

SEX &
LOVE
&MARRIAGE
&KIDS

THE BEST OF IRISH HUMOR

Two married friends are out drinking.
One says to the other,
"I can never sneak into the house after I've been drinking. I've tried everything. I turn the headlights off before I go in the driveway. I shut off the engine and coast into the garage. I take my shoes off and creep upstairs. I undress in the bathroom. I do everything I can think of, but my wife still yells at me for staying out so late."
The friend replies: "Do what I do. I screech into the driveway, slam the front door, stomp up the stairs, throw my shoes into the closet, jump into bed, slap my wife's ass and say loudly, 'WHO WANTS TO GET LAID?'
"She always pretends she's asleep."

Katie says, "Liam, we've been married a long time. You're good looking and I think you've slept with a lot of women. I won't be mad, but I want to know how many."
Liam says,
"My lovely lass, I never slept with anyone but you.
"All the rest, I was awake."

There are no new sins, but the old ones get more publicity.

"Someday I'd like a little brother," said a young lad to his friend.
 "There's only so much you can blame on a dog."

A small boy got lost at the supermarket in Dublin. He came up to a guard and said, "I've lost my Dad."
"What's he like?" asked the guard.
"Beer and women," said the boy.

Finn's wife had been killed in an accident.
"Did she say anything before she died?" asked a policeman.
She spoke without interruption for about forty years," said Finn.

Years ago, a shy young woman went to deliver her first baby.
When the doctor said to remove her pants, well, she would have none of that! The doctor said, "Seems to me you've already removed them too often before now!"

Walking into the pub, Tim said to the bartender, "Pour me a stiff one, Sean. I just had another tiff with the little woman."
"Did you now? And how did this one end?"
"Well I'll tell ya...when it was over, herself came to me on her hands and knees, she did." "You don't say! Now there's a switch! What did she say?"
She said, 'Come out from under that bed, you gutless weasel!'"

A man and his wife were in a Belfast hospital after the birth of another child. The doctor came in and said they should abstain from sex for a week. The fella said, "Geez, doc, you should have told me that twenty minutes ago."

Casey's wife, Maureen, sat at his bedside while he lay dying. Weakly, he said, "I've something I must confess before I die."
I must tell that I slept with your sister, mother, and best friend, not to mention—"
"Shhh, I know," she said. "Now just rest and let the poison work."

An Irish daughter went to America and suddenly returned after five years. Upon seeing her, her father lost his temper. "Where's have ye been all this time? Why did ye not write to us, not even a line? Why didn't ye call? Can ye not understand what ye put yer old Mother through?"
The girl, crying, replied: "Oh, Dad...sniff, sniff...how can I tell you? Dad, I became a prostitute."
"Ye what?!! Out of here, ye shameless harlot! Sinner! Yer a disgrace to this Catholic family!"
"Okay, Dad. As you wish," she replied, tears running down her cheeks. "I just came back to give Mum this fur coat and this title deed to a ten bedroom mansion. For me little brother, this gold Rolex. And for you, Daddy, the new Mercedes Limited Edition convertible that's parked outside and... well, I wanted you all to spend New Year's Eve on board my new yacht in the Riviera..." She took in a deep breath.
"Hold on! What was it ye said ye'd become?"

The girl, crying again, said, "A prostitute, Daddy! Oh dear, can you ever forgive me?" "Oh beJesus! Ye scared me half to death, girl! I thought ye said a Protestant! Come here and give yer old Dad a hug now!"

He gave her a zirconia ring when he proposed. She called him a cheapskate. "It was in honor of St. Patrick's Day," said he. "It's a sham rock."

There was a young lady at sea
Who said, "Gawd. But it hurts me to pee."
""I see," said the mate.
"That accounts for the state
Of the captain, the purser, and me."

A lady athletic and handsome
Got wedged in her sleeping room transom.
When she offered much gold,
For release, she was told
That the view was worth more than the ransom.

If you can't laugh at trouble, you'll have nothing to laugh at when you're old.

[143]

Mrs. McGervey was walking in Dublin when she met up with Father O'Flaherty. The Father said, "The top of the morning to ye. Aren't you Mrs. McGervey and didn't I marry ye two years ago?"

"Aye, that ye did, Father."

The priest asked, "And be there any wee little ones?" "No, not yet, Father," she replied.

The priest said, "Well now, I'm going to Rome next week and I'll light a candle for ye and yer husband."

"Oh thank ye, Father." And they parted ways.

Ten years later, they met again. The priest said, "Well now, Mrs. McGervey, how are ye these days?"

"Oh, very well, Father."

"And have ye any wee little ones yet?"

She replied, "Oh, yes, Father. Three sets of twins and four singles, ten in all!"

"Why, bless ye, that's wonderful! And how is yer husband doin'?"

"He's gone to Rome to blow out your damned candle!"

"So, Mrs. Connery, you want a divorce?" the solicitor questioned his new client. "Tell me about it. Do you have a grudge?"

"Oh no," said the woman. "Sure now, we have a carport."

The solicitor tried again. "Well, does the man beat you up?"

"No, no," said Mrs. Connery, looking puzzled. "I'm always first out of bed."

Still hopeful, the solicitor tried again. "Does he go in for unnatural connubial practices?"

"Sure now, he plays the flute but I don't think he knows anything about the connubial."

Now desperate, the solicitor pushed on. "What I'm trying to find out are what grounds you have."

"Bless you, sor, we live in a flat. Not even a window box, let alone grounds."

"Mrs. Connery," the solicitor said, in complete frustration, "you need a reason for the court to consider divorce. What is the reason?"

"Ah, well now," she said, "sure it's because the man can't hold an intelligent conversation."

Kevin O'Hara walked into a pub in Tipperary, went to the bar and ordered a glass of Guinness.

"Certainly," said the bartender, "and that'll be one cent."

"One cent? You can't mean that!"

"It's a special today. Perhaps you'd like a look at our menu and see if there's something you'd like to eat."

"How much for the sirloin and a bottle of red?" asked O'Hara. "Five cents," says the barman.

"Five cents? Does it cost five cents for every customer in here today?"

 "Yes, sir."

O'Hara couldn't quite believe this, so he turned to the other customers at the bar and said, "Is this true?"

They all hoisted their glasses and agreed.

"I'd like to speak to the owner of this place," he said.

"Oh, he's upstairs with my wife."

"What's he doing upstairs with your wife?"

The bartender replied with a grim smile:

"The same thing I'm doing to his business down here."

An American lady tourist is having a walk on the Cliffs of Mohr in County Clare, when she comes upon an Irish piper, resplendent in his kilts and sash, passed out cold on the grass, his bagpipes near his side.
She wonders if the man wears anything under his kilts, so she tiptoes over, takes a peek, and oh dear, he is certainly naked.
She ties a ribbon from her purse around his penis and leaves.
When the man wakes up, he needs to relieve himself and sees the ribbon.
"I don't know where you've been or what you've done," he says.
"But I'm glad you got first prize!"

Little Katie gets home from school and tells her Mammy that the boys were asking her to do cartwheels.
Mammy said, "Don't do it. The boys only want to see your knickers."
Katy said, "I know.
That's why I hid them in me backpack."

Sign over the mirror in a pub bathroom:
No wonder you always go home alone!

[147]

McClinty's bride came down the aisle and when she reached the altar, she saw her husband-to-be standing there with his golf bag by his side.

She said, "What are your golf clubs doing here?"

He answered, "This isn't going to take all day, is it?"

Maura and Kathleen meet at the market. They haven't seen each other for some time. Maura asks after Kathleen's husband. Kathleen says,

"I'm sorry to say that Brian died last week. He went out to the garden to get a cabbage for our dinner, had a heart attack, and...well, that was that."

"Sweet Mother Mary!" exclaimed Maura. "I'm so sorry! Whatever did you do?"

"Oh, I opened a tin of peas instead."

Murphy told Quinn that his wife was driving him to drink.

Quinn felt he had a pretty nice deal. His wife made him walk.

Maeve walked into the kitchen to find her husband with a fly swatter and a look of concentration.
"What are you doing?" "Hunting flies."
"Really? Kill any?" "Yes. Three males and two females."
"How do you know the sex of a fly?"
"Easy. Three were on a beer can and two were on the phone."

A young couple on their wedding night were in the honeymoon suite.
As they were undressing, the husband, a big burly man, took off his trousers and tossed them over to her. "Put these on," he said. "I want you to wear them" Well, of course, they could have gone around her twice.
"I can't wear your trousers!" she said.
"Good that you know that," he answered.
"Just remember it. I wear the trousers in this family."
Now she flipped him her knickers and said, "Here, put these on, why don't you?"
"I can't get into your knickers!"
"That's right and that's how it will stay until you change your attitude."

A nice respectable lady walked into the pharmacy, looked straight into the pharmacist's eyes and said, "I'd like to buy some cyanide."

"Why in the world would you want something like that?"

"I need it to poison my husband."

The pharmacist turned red and he exclaimed: "I can't be giving you cyanide to kill your husband! It's against the law! The Garda will surely come after me and they'll throw both of us into jail! Absolutely NOT!"

The lady reached into her purse and pulled out a picture of a man in bed with the pharmacist's wife.

"That's my husband," she said.

The pharmacist studied the photo and then said, "Well, now, to be sure that's a different thing. You didn't say you had a prescription."

When Danny boy found out he was going to inherit a fortune when his sickly father died, he decided he should find a woman to share this windfall with.

One evening he went to a pub where he spotted a gorgeous young woman with flaming red hair and a drop-dead body.
"I may look like just an ordinary fella," he said as he walked up to her. "But in a short while, I'll be inheriting millions of pounds."
Impressed, she went home with him that evening.
Three days later, she became his stepmother.
Women really ARE smarter than men.

Kevin and Moira, being good Irish Catholics, had so many children, they didn't know what to do. Kevin says to Moira, "Sure, and we got to get some advice from the parish priest. We can't keep on with any more children."
So they went to talk with the priest and the priest says to Kevin, "Now, me boyo, as you know, the Church only allows two ways to limit the wee ones. One is to abstain altogether and the other is the rhythm."
Kevin scratches his head and says, "Well and good, Father, but where am I going to find a Kelly band at 4:00 o'clock in the morning?"

[151]

A young Dublin married couple enjoyed a full sex life, and the woman became used to rewarding him between the sheets. But he wanted to prove to her that he wanted her for more than just sex, so one day he brought her a huge bouquet of flowers.
"They're lovely," she said and then added, "And I suppose you expect me to spend the weekend on my back with my legs apart?"
"Why?" he asked her.
"Don't we have a vase any more?"

On their wedding night, Mike's bride lies down spread-eagled on the bed.
"I guess you know what I want," says she.
"The entire bed, it looks like," says Mike.

For those two little birds in the tree,
Or for rabbits and cat, you'll agree,
To mate female with male
Is the point of life's tale.
So why this reluctance with me?

Sighed a newlywed damsel of Wheeling:
"A honeymoon sounds so appealing.
But for nearly two weeks
I've heard only bed squeaks,
And seen nothing but cracks in the ceiling!"

An observant young man of the West
Said: "I've found out by personal test,
That men who make passes
At girls who wear glasses,
Get just as well laid as the rest."

A buxom young steno named Baines
At her work took particular pains.
But the principal feature
Of this charming young creature
Was she ran more to bosom than brains.

There was a young lady from Byer
Whose hemlines got higher and higher.
But the size of her thighs
Provoked merely surprise,
And extinguished the flames of desire.

An out-of-touch lassie from Cork
Would use neither spoon, knife, or fork.
And when she was wedded
She would not be bedded,
Since babies are brought by the stork.

There was a young friar from Galway
Who took two nuns and ran away.
They lived on an isthmus.
The one he called Christmas
And the other? Well maybe one day.

There was a young fellow named Baker
Who seduced a lively young Quaker.
And when he had done it,
She straightened her bonnet
And said, "I give thanks to my maker."

Said Napoleon, Emperor Supreme,
While scouting about for a queen:
"I'd much rather squeeza
Maria Louisa
Than sleep with that bitch Josephine."

It seems a young damsel from Spencer
Than whom few young damsels are denser,
Was beguiled by the flattery
Of the Irishman Slattery...
What later occurred we must censor.

Clancy went into the confessional and said to the priest, "I almost had an affair with another woman."
"What do you mean—almost?"
"Well, we got undressed and rubbed together but then I stopped."
Said the priest, "Rubbing is the same as putting it in. Say five Hail Mary's and put $50 in the poor box."
Clancy left the confessional, paused a moment by the poor box, then started to leave.
The priest, who was watching him, ran to him saying,
"I saw that. You didn't put any money in the poor box."
"True," said Clancy,
"But I rubbed $50 on the box and according to you that's the same as putting it in."

Maureen came to the newspaper to pay for her husband's obit. She had written one out but the editor told her it would be ten pounds. She told the editor she had only two pounds, and he said that was enough for two words.
So she chose, "Pete died."
Told she could have three more for free, she wrote out: "Pete died. Boat for sale."

Six friends were playing poker when one of them suddenly died. "I'll tell his wife," said Brian. He went to their house and said, "Your husband lost a lot of money and is afraid to come home."
 "Tell him to drop dead!" said she.
 "All right, I will," he said.

Ronan O'Riley finally came up to bed at 3:00 in the morning.
"Why were you up so late?" his wife asked.
"It's the cat's fault."
"The cat's fault?"
"I was waitin' for her to come home so I could put her out for the night."

Mary Margaret, a good Irish wife, said to her husband, Sweeny: "You've been so good about staying away from the pub and that, I want to do something special for ya. I saw, when we was in France, how much you enjoyed them escargots. You go to the fish store and get us some and I'll make 'em up." The thought of the garlicky escargots made Sweeny's mouth water. On his way, he had to pass the pub. As he hurried by, all his cronies yelled out to him, "Hey there, Sweeny, come in and let us buy you a pint!" "No, no, no," he said. "I promised ..." They insisted. "No, no, no," insisted Sweeny. Then: "Well...just one. Soon as I go to the fish store."

It was 11:00 PM when Sweeny checked his watch in the pub. "Oh, no!" he groaned. He grabbed the escargots and left the pub running. He got to his gate and then tripped and the snails went flying everywhere. Mary Margaret came out in her nightie and yelled "Sweeny! It's nearly midnight!" Sweeny got to his feet, waving his arms at the snails. "Come on boys, keep it going," he hollered. "WE'RE ALMOST THERE!"

[157]

Old Seamus Slattery is dying and the neighbor women are downstairs with his wife, Agnes, cooking for the wake.
Old Seamus suddenly comes to and calls for his wife. "It's himself!" says the surprised Agnes, who hurries up the stairs.
"Seamus, darling, what is it?"
He says, "Is that a ham I smell cooking down there?"
"Oh, aye, a fine big ham."
"And did you put the cloves to it and cover it with mustard?"
"Oh, aye, just the way you like it."
"And would you be after cutting me a wee piece of that ham?"
"Oh Seamus, what a joker you are! You know we can't put knife to that ham until the wake!"

O'Donnell came upon McMurphy, sitting in the pub, looking distressed. When asked what the problem was, McMurphy said, "My wife enrolled me in a bridge club." "That's not so bad," said O'Donnell. "I didn't think so, either," said McMurphy, "until I found I'm scheduled to jump off next Tuesday."

[158]

A small farmer was interviewed by the Department of Pensions inspector who claimed he wasn't paying proper wages.

"I need a list of your employees and how much you pay them," said the inspector.

"Well, there's my farm hand who's been with me for three years. I pay him two hundred a week plus free room and board. The lady who cleans and cooks, she's been here for 18 months and I pay her 150 a week plus free room and board.

"Then there's the half-wit. He works about 18 hours every day and does about 90% of all the work. He makes about ten pounds a week, pays his own room and board, and I buy him a bottle of whisky every Saturday night. He also sleeps with my wife."

"That's the man I want to talk to ... the half-wit," said the inspector.

"That would be me, then," said the farmer.

Miss Flannigan was nearing 35 and had no prospects of marrying. She put an ad in the paper that said, simply, HUSBAND WANTED. Two days later, she had over 100 replies, and they all said: YOU CAN HAVE MINE.

John O'Riley hoisted his beer and said,
"Here's to spending the rest of me life
between the legs of me wife!"
That won him top prize at the local pub for
Best Toast of the Year.
The proud John went home that night and
told his wife, Mary Kate, who asked, "Aye,
did ye now? Well, what was your toast."
O'Riley swallowed hard. Mary Kate might
not like him talking about sex with her in the
pub. So he said, "Here's to spending the
rest of me life sitting in church beside me
wife."
"Oh, and that is very nice indeed, John,"
said a beaming Mary Kate.
The next day, Mary Kate ran into one of
John's drinking buddies. The man chuckled
and grinned at her. "You know that John
won the big prize with a toast to you," he
said, in a teasing tone.
She said, "Aye, he told me, and I was a bit
surprised, too. You know, he's only been in
there twice in the last four years. Once, I
had to pull him by the ears to make him
come and the other time, he fell asleep."

When Kennedy showed up at Mass one Sunday, the priest was amazed. The man had never been to church in his life.

After Mass, he said to Kennedy, "What made ya come to church after all this time?"

"I gotta be honest with you, Father. Awhile back, I misplaced me hat and I really, really love that hat. I know that Murphy has a hat just like it. I'm ashamed to say I was planning to go to where he always leaves his hat at the back of the church, and steal it."

"Well, I notice that you didn't do such a sinful thing. What made you change your mind?"

"Well, Father, it was your sermon on the Ten Commandments did it."

With a tear in his eye, the priest gave Kennedy a big smile and said, "After I talked about 'Thou Shalt Not Steal' you decided you would rather do without your hat than burn eternally in Hell?"

Kennedy shook his head. "No, Father, it was after you talked about 'Thou Shalt Not Commit Adultery.'

"I remembered where I left me hat."

Murphy walks into Mick's barn and sees Mick dancing naked in front of his tractor.
"Jesus, Joseph and Mary!" he exclaims.
"What are you doin'?"
"Well," says Mick, "me and Bridey haven't been getting on too well lately; so I went to a top doctor and he says I should do something sexy to a tractor."

Dan Malloy and his pregnant wife live on a farm in a distant rural region. There's no running water, no electricity, no mod cons. One night Mrs. Malloy goes into labor and the doctor comes.
"What can I do?" asks Dan.
"Hold the lantern, Danny boy. Ah and here it comes! A fine strapping boy!"
"Saints be praised—" Dan begins but the doctor says, "Wait a minute. Hold the lantern, Dan." A few minutes later, he holds up another newborn. Dan begins to thank God, when the doctor cuts in. "Wait! And hold the lantern! Yes, it's another boy!' He holds the child up for Dan's inspection.
"Doctor," says Dan. "Do you think it's the light attracting them?"

An Irish mother was congratulated by the Pope on having 17 sons.

"And every time a boy, eh?" said the Pope.

"No, sir," she replied. "Lot of times we got nothing."

There was a young fellow of Keating
Whose pride took a terrible beating.
That happens to males
When they learn the details
Of their wives' extramarital cheating.

Said the newlyweds staying at Kitely:
"We turn off the electric lights nightly.
'Tis best of embark
Upon sex in the dark—
The <u>look</u> of the thing's so unsightly!"

Try our Rubber Girl Friend (air-inflatable)
Perennially young (quite insatiable.)
Our satisfied clients,
From mere midgets to giants,
Say she's incredibly sexy and mateable.

There was a man from Belfast who thought Little Red Riding Hood was a condom.

Danny was stumped. His wife's birthday
was coming up in two days and he still
hadn't figured out what to get her as a gift.
His buddy Kevin said, "You should write up a
certificate, all fancy and that, saying she can
have two hours of great sex any way she
wants it. She'll probably be thrilled."
Danny had to agree. So he did it just as
Kevin had described.
The day after her birthday, Kevin asked,
"Well, did you do it? How did it turn out?"
"She loved it!" said Danny. "She jumped up
and thanked me, kissed me on the mouth,
and ran out the door yelling, "See you in a
couple of hours!"

Mary Flaherty's late husband was a
notorious criminal, but she loved him. He
died a year ago and she hasn't visited his
grave. So she goes to the cemetery and
looks for it. No Kevin Flaherty. She asks the
cemetery director, who looks through all the
books. "Sorry," he says, "the only Flaherty I
see is a Mary Flaherty."
"Ah, yes," says Mary. "Of course.
"Everything was in my name."

It seems that Murphy, who is 88, is feeling poorly all of a sudden. So his son Joe takes him to the doctor. The doctor gives Murphy a complete head-to-toe examination, then asks to see them both.

"I've some bad news for you, Murphy. Your heart's given out. You have two months."

Murphy is stunned. He says to Joe, "Well, it's not good news but I've had a full life and if the Lord wants me, well...I'll go. But first I'm after having me a few pints with me mates at Mike Hannigan's pub."

At the pub, Hannigan says, "And how are you feeling today, Murphy?"

"Not good, Mike. I've been to the doctor and he says I've only two more months."

"What a shame," says Hannigan. "And what's ailin' ya?"

"It's the AIDs," says Murphy.

On their way home an hour or so later, Joe says, "Da, why did you tell everyone you have the AIDs? It's a heart condition that's killin' ya."

"Sure don't I know that," says Murphy. "But I want to be sure none of those old buggers try sleeping with your Ma when I'm gone."

What's the disease that paralyzes some
women from the waist down?
Marriage.

What did God say after creating man?
I can do better.

Patrick Mullens was in court for non payment
of maintenance to his ex-wife. The judge
told Patrick, "I'm increasing this allowance
and giving your wife 50 pounds per week."
"That's grand," said Patrick. "And I might
send her a few bob meself."

Michael Houlihan was courting Frances
Phelan. The young couple sat in the parlor
of the girl's house night after night, much to
the annoyance of old man Phelan.
One night, he couldn't take any more.
Standing at the top of the stairs, he yelled
down, "What's that young fella still doin'
here all hours of the night?" "Why, Dad,"
Frances said, "Michael was just telling me
everything that's in his heart!" "Well, next
time," roared Phelan, "let him tell you what's
in his head; it won't take half as long!"

A man walking down a Galway street catches a cab just going by.

He gets into the taxi and the cabbie says: "Perfect timing, begorrah. Just like Mick Murphy."

Passenger: "Who?"

Cabbie: "Mick Murphy. Luck o' the Irish he had, did everything right all the time. When he needed a cab, one would come right along...like you today."

Passenger: "Well, he must have had some bad luck from time to time. Nobody's perfect."

Cabbie: "Mick Murphy was perfect. He played golf like an old pro, sang 'Oh Danny Boy' better than John McCormack, and danced? Oh he was a regular Fred Astaire, he was!"

Passenger: "Sounds really special."

Cabbie: "Oh and he really knew how to treat a woman, did Mick. Little gifts, back rubs, special dinners...you name it."

Passenger: An amazing fellow. How did you know him?

Cabbie: "I never met him. He died and I married his freaking wife!"

[167]

An Irishman, an Englishman and a Scot were sitting in the pub, drinking and discussing how stupid their wives were.

The Brit said, "My wife is so stupid. Last week she went to the supermarket and bought 100 euros worth of meat because it was on sale; and we don't have a big freezer." The Scotsman agreed that sounded pretty thick but said, "My wife is even thicker. Just last week she went and spent 10,000 euro on a new car. And she can't drive!"

The Irishman threw back the last of his Guinness. "My wife just left to go on a holiday in Greece. I watched her packing her bag, and she must have put about 100 condoms in there. And she doesn't even have a penis!"

After a heavy rainstorm, a mother saw her 5-year-old son shoving the face of his little brother into a big puddle. Angrily, she went out to rescue the little one.

"But Mammy, we was just playing church. I baptized him in the name of the Father, the son, and into the hole he goes!"

Three confirmed bachelors from County Clare decided to take wives.

Sean, the first man, married a Greek girl. He told her he expected her to keep the house clean and do the dishes. It took a couple of days, but on the third day he came home to see everything done as he liked.

Kevin, the second, married a Thai girl. He gave his wife orders that she was to do the all the cleaning and dishwashing, and cook dinner every evening. It took a couple of days but on the third day, everything was as he wanted it.

Brian, the third man, married an Irish girl. He told her he expected her to keep the house clean, dishes washed, lawn mowed, laundry done, and hot meals on the table for every meal.

The first day he didn't see anything, the second day he didn't see anything, either; but by the third day, some of the swelling had gone down, and he could see out of his left eye and his arm was healed enough that he could fix himself a sandwich and load the dishwasher.

He still has some difficulty when he urinates.

Seamus and his wife walked past a swanky new restaurant in Belfast last night.
"Did you smell that food?" said his wife. "Incredible!"
Being a nice guy, Seamus thought, "What the heck, I'll treat her."
So they turned and walked past it again.

'So have you figured what to get your wife for Christmas, Pat?'
"Well, she said she wanted something with diamonds on it.
"So I got her a pack of cards."

Patrick was at the Rugby World Cup.
In the packed stadium, there was only one seat, the one next to him.
"Whose seat is that?" asked his neighbor.
"Me wife's"
"But why isn't she here?"
"She died."
"So why didn't you give the ticket to one of your friends?"
"They're all at the funeral."

What is a zebra? 26 sizes up from an A bra.

[170]

Farmer Dowd's truck was in the shop so he walked home. On the way, he bought a bucket, a gallon of paint, a pair of chickens and a goose. Now the problem was how to carry all of this home. While he was cogitating, an attractive older woman asked for directions to an address and, as it was close to his farm, he offered to walk her there. But he admitted he wasn't sure how to carry all he had bought.
The woman said, "Put the can of paint in the bucket. Carry the bucket in one hand, put a chicken under each arm, and the goose in your other hand." Well, it was a good idea. On the way, Dowd suggested they take his shortcut down a deserted alley.
The woman said, "I'm a lonely widow with no one to protect me. How do I know you won't push me against the wall and have your way with me?"
Dowd said, "Bejeezus, how could I possibly do that with all this that I'm carrying?"
With a small smile, she said,
"Set the goose down, cover him with the bucket, put the can of paint on top of the bucket, and I'll hold the chickens."

[171]

The only cow in Ballymena stopped giving milk. The townfolk found they could buy a cow in Scotland quite cheaply. Scotland not being too far, three fellows went and bought it and brought it back. It was a lovely cow and gave copious amounts of milk.

Everyone was happy. They decided to buy a bull so they could get more cows and never run out of milk again.

They put the bull in the pasture with the cow but whenever he tried to mount her, the cow would move away. The bull tried every which way to approach the cow and she always moved to avoid him.

The vet was called to watch this bovine drama. He pondered and then asked if by any chance this was a cow from Scotland. "How in the world did you know we got the cow in Scotland?" they asked the vet.

With a distant look in his eye, the vet replied: "My wife is from Scotland."

"You don't deserve a wife like me!" screamed Brenda Doyle at her husband. "I don't deserve a toothache, either, but I've got it!" he yelled back.

A young lad went around to his girlfriend's house to talk with her father.

"I'd like your daughter's hand in marriage," he said.

The father thought for a moment, then replied: "Take all of her, or nothing!"

A couple from Dublin were having an argument and the husband said to his wife, "D'ya know, I was a complete eejit when I married you!"

The irate wife replied: "That's right, but I was in love and didn't notice."

Nora called the police to report her husband missing. "He's 6'2" tall, red curly hair, and a smile that makes everyone love him," she said tearfully. The police put up a notice on every tree and telephone pole.

Kathleen, Nora's next-door neighbor called the police and said, "That's not Brian at all. He's a wee fella with a tooth missing in front. She's lying."

When contronted, Nora said, "Just because I reported him missing doesn't mean I want him back."

LETTER TO THE OBSTETRICIAN

Dear Doctor, I'd like to apply for an operation to make me sterile. After being married for seven years, and having a child each year, I've come to the conclusion that contraceptives are useless.

When we were first married, we were told to use the rhythm method. Whilst trying the samba and the tango, my wife fell pregnant and I ruptured myself doing the cha-cha.

A doctor then suggested we use the safe period. At this time we were living with in-laws and had to wait three weeks for a safe period, when the house was empty. That did not work.

An old aunt informed us that if we made love while breast feeding we would be alright. It hardly tastes like Guinness, but I finished up with clear skin, silky hair and another child on the way.

Another old wives' tale said if my wife jumped up and down after sex, this would prevent pregnancy. After breast feeding (see above) she would have ended up with two black eyes.

I asked our chemist about the condom. He demonstrated how easy it was to use so I bought a packet. My wife fell pregnant again, which doesn't surprise me, as I fail to see how plastic stretched over the thumb can prevent a baby.

The Dutch cap came next. We were very hopeful of this and it didn't interfere with our sex life at all. But begorrah, didn't it give my wife a severe headache! We were given the largest size, but it was still too tight across her forehead.

Finally we tried the pill. At first it kept falling out; then we realized we were doing it wrong. My wife started putting it between her knees, thus preventing me from getting anywhere near her. This did work for a while until the night she forgot it and another child resulted.

You must appreciate my problem. If this operation is unsuccessful, I'll have to revert to oral sex. Although I don't mind just talking about it, it could never be as good as the real thing.

Yours sincerely
Mac Murphy

A married couple were asleep when the phone rang at two in the morning. The wife picked up the phone, listened a moment, and said, "How should I know? That's 200 miles from here!" She hung up.
"Who was that?" asked the husband.
"I really don't know. Some woman wanting to know if the coast was clear."

A doctor in Galway was on his early morning walk, when he noticed a very elderly woman sitting in her front garden. She was quite bent, totally wrinkled, yet she was smoking a cigar and smiling.
He walked up to her and said, "I'm a doctor and couldn't help noticing how contented you look. What's your secret?"
"Ten cigars a day," she answered. "Before bed, I smoke a nice big joint. Apart from that, I drink a whole bottle of the best whisky every week, and I can't forget the Guinness I take with every meal. And, no, I don't exercise. I have sex regularly instead."
"That is absolutely amazing! Tell me, how old are you?"
"Thirty-four," she replied.

[176]

Seamus and Murphy were only a year short of retirement; but that didn't keep Murphy from bragging about his sexual endurance. "Three times in one night. Begorrah, but that's a miracle," said Seamus. "How'd you do it?"

"Easy," said Murphy. "We made love, then I rolled over and took a ten-minute nap. When I woke up, we did it again and I took another ten-minute nap. And then we did it a third time. And I woke up this morning feeling like a bull... me, at my age!"

Seamus said, "I gotta try that. Me wife won't believe what's happening." That night he made love to his wife, took a ten-minute nap, made love again, took another nap, did a third round, then rolled over and fell sound asleep. He woke up in the morning, feeling young again, and ran to the factory, where he found his boss waiting outside for him.

"What's this?" said Seamus. "For twenty years I've worked here and never been late once. Now you're holding twenty minutes against me?"

"What twenty minutes? Where were you on Tuesday and Wednesday?"

Women at a marriage seminar were asked how long it had been since they said "I love you" to their husbands. The answers were depressing. So the seminar leader told them to get their cell phones and text to their husbands, "I love you, sweetheart." The women were then told to exchange phones and to read aloud the text message responses.

Here are some of the replies from the men:

"Who is this?"

"Eh, mother of my children, are you sick?"

"What now? Did you crash the car again?"

"I don't understand what you mean?"

"Don't be beating about the bush. Just tell me how much you need."

"If you don't tell me who this message is really for, someone will die."

"Am I dreaming?"

"Your mother is coming to stay, isn't she?"

"I thought we agreed that we would not drink during the day."

"What did you do now?"

"?!?!"

And, at last, one good response:

"I love you, too."

[178]

Connery came home from a hard day in the potato fields, longing for a hot dinner.
He said to his wife, "Darlin', couldn't we skip the frozen dinners that you put into the microwave and have a real home-cooked dinner tonight?"
"Of course, my love," says she. "I'll just open some tins."

Miss O'Grundy was standing in front of her class giving an English grammar lesson.
"Now, class," she said, "Consider this sentence: 'I didn't have no fun last weekend.' Who can tell me how to fix that?"
Little Patrick in the front row raised his hand, and said:
"Get yourself a boyfriend, Miss."

Bridey was unhappy when, once again, her husband Brian came home drunk and sprawled onto the floor. "Enough of this!" she shouted. "Why d'you always have to come home half drunk from that pub of yours?" Brian hiccupped and turned his head to stare at her with bleared eyes.
"Because I run out of money," he mumbled.

[179]

Kevin was busy digging a hole at a Galway building site, when his foreman came up and asked if he'd like to buy a raffle ticket.

"What for?" asked Kevin.

"You know the crane operator, Higgins, who died suddenly last week?"

"Yes, I do."

"Well, it's for his wife and five kids."

"Oh then, thanks very much but no thanks. I've already got a wife and four kids of my own. I don't need to win any more."

Dylan O'Brien, eleven years old, comes home from school one day and tells his Da he has a part in the school play.

"That's grand, son," says his father. "What will you be playin'?"

"I'm the husband in an Irish family."

"Oh, that's no good," says Dylan's Da. "Go back and tell your teacher you want a <u>speaking</u> part."

The widow sat expectantly in the solicitor's office for the reading of the will. It said, "I, James Connelly, being of sound mind, spent all my money before I died."

A doctor and his wife were having an argument at the breakfast table. The husband got up in a rage and shouted, "What's more, you're no good in bed, either!" and stormed out of the house. Some hours later, he realized he probably shouldn't have said that. He called home to apologize.

After many many rings, his wife finally picked up the phone. Now irritated, the husband said, "What took you so long to answer?"

"I was in bed."

"At this hour? In bed? Whatever for?"

"Getting a second opinion."

Nora O'Toole was preparing pancakes for her two sons, Sean and Seamus.

The boys began to argue about who would get the first pancake off the griddle.

Said Nora: "If Jesus were here, he'd say, 'Give the first pancake to my brother. I can wait.'"

Seamus turned to his younger brother. "Sean...you be Jesus."

Michael and Mary Connelly, in their 60s, were celebrating a wedding anniversary. On that special day, a leprechaun came to them and said they had been so good and loyal, each could have one wish.
Mary wished for a trip around the world with her husband. Whoosh! Instantly she had airline and cruise tickets in her hands.
Michael wishes for a female companion 30 years young than himself. Whoosh! Instantly he turned 90.
That was a grand leprechaun, wasn't it?

Young Patrick brought three girls home for his Mammy to meet. They were all curvaceous, sweet-faced, and pretty and they all had red hair.
"Mammy, I plan to marry one of these lovely young girls. Can you guess which one?"
Without missing a beat, she said, "The one in the middle."
Patrick was dumbfounded.
"But they're so much the same! How could you know so quickly?"
"Because I don't like her!" snapped Mammy.

[182]

Brenda O'Malley awoke during the night and saw that her husband, Sean, was not in bed. She went downstairs and found him, teary-eyed, sitting at the kitchen table with a glass of scotch. She asked what the trouble was. "Remember," said Sean, "when we were first seeing each other and your father caught us in the car, making love?"
Touched, she said, "Of course I do, darlin'."
"Do you remember when he threatened me and said, 'Either you marry my daughter or spend twenty years in jail?'"
"I do, of course I do."
He blinked some tears away and in a voice shaking with emotion, said: "I would have gotten out today."

Five-year-old Mary Clare came home at the end of her first week of school and announced: "I'm not going back there, Mammy. I can't read and I can't write and they don't let me talk."

Married-women exercise. Banging your head against the wall uses 150 calories an hour.

A widow getting on in years had an elderly boyfriend who visited her twice a year.
After their January tryst, he got dressed and said, "I'll see you in July."
"Don't you ever think of anything but sex?" she said.

Patrick says he thinks priests ought to be allowed to marry. That way, they'll know what Hell is really like!

Maura is pregnant for the first time. She asks her doctor what position she should be in when she gives birth.
The doctor says, "The same one you were in when you conceived this child."
"You mean," asked Maura, "I have to go to Lovers Lane and dangle my feet out the car window for an hour?"

Two women in Galway were having tea in a café when a nattily-dressed man walked by.
"He certainly dresses well," said Nora.
"And so quickly, too," added Colleen.

Stalemate: a leading cause of divorce.

God told Adam, "I'm giving you ten years for your sex life. Adam complained that he really needed more.

God said, "If I give you something, don't complain. I'm really busy now. We'll talk later." And he left.

God went to the lion and said, "You can have twenty years of sex." The lion said, "I really only need ten years." Adam said, "I'll take those ten years, and gladly." God agreed.

God gave the monkey twenty years of a sex life and the monkey, too, said he needed only ten. Adam raised his hand and God nodded his agreement.

Before the end of the day, Adam had ten more years the donkey didn't want and ten more from the parrot.

That may go far in explaining why men have ten normal years of sex, ten years of lion about it, ten years of monkeying around, ten years of being an ass about it, and the final ten years talking about it!

How do university men propose marriage? "You're going to have a <u>what</u>?"

Nora informed her little boy that his shoes were on the wrong feet.
"Oh, no, Mammy," he said. "I'm sure they're my feet."

Ciaran walked into the pub with a puppy.
"What a grand looking dog that is," said his friend Niall.
Ciaran smiled. "I got him for me wife."
Said Niall: "Seems a fair swap."

When the collection plate comes around at church on Sunday, little Molly whispers loudly, "Don't pay for me, Da. I'm under five."

Birthdays are good for you. The more you have the longer you live.

Danny Doyle returned from the pub one night to a torrent of abuse from his wife.
"If you spent one-half of the time at home," she moaned, "as you spend in that pub, I think I'd fall down dead!"
"There, now," chided Danny. "No use in trying to bribe me, now!"

[186]

KERRYMAN AND PADDY JOKES

THE BEST OF IRISH HUMOR

A Kerryman found himself in the Underground late one night. He saw a sign saying DOGS MUST BE CARRIED ON THE MOVING STAIRS.
"Now where do they expect me to find a dog at this hour?" he complained.

How do you recognize a Kerryman on an oil rig?
He's the one throwing crusts of bread to the helicopters.

A fellow walked into a bar in Dublin and asked the barman if he had heard the latest Kerryman joke.
"I'm warning you," said the barman. "I'm a Kerryman meself."
"That's all right," said the fellow.
"I'll tell it very slowly."

You know it's a Kerry pirate when he has a patch over each eye.

I was asked on a test what is found in cells. Apparently, "Kerrymen" wasn't the correct answer.

Paddy and Mikie went on a holiday to France and stayed at a country farmhouse.
They were disgusted to find that everyone, even the kids, spoke French.
One morning, they were awakened by a cock crowing. "D'you know?" said one to the other, "that's the first word of English we've heard spoken since we got here!"

Don't worry what Kerrymen might think. They don't do it very often.

A businessman hired a Kerryman to take phone calls in the office. One day, the phone rang and the Kerryman answered, spoke a few words, and hung up. "Who was that?" asked the boss. "Oh, some fellow saying it was a long distance from New York. I told him everybody knew that."

A Kerryman went to see a show and one of the acts was a ventriloquist who told one Kerryman joke after the other.
"Look!" shouted the Kerryman, standing up in the audience.
"I'm fed up being insulted by all these jokes. We aren't as stupid as you make out."

[190]

"Please sit down," said the ventriloquist. "After all, they're only jokes and don't tell me that Kerrymen haven't got a sense of humor!"
"I'm not talking to you," said the Kerryman. "I'm talking to the little fellow on your knee."

Paddy rang Aer Lingus and asked how long it took to fly from Dublin to London.
"Just a moment, sir," said the girl on the desk.
"Thank you," said Paddy and hung up.

Paddy was picked up on a rape charge. He was placed in a lineup with ten other fellows and the accusing woman was escorted into the room.
Paddy jumped forward and yelled, "That's her! That's her! I'd recognize her anywhere!"

Why do Kerrymen always carry a little rubbish in their pockets?
Identification.

Two Kerrymen hired an open cockpit aeroplane to fly over Dublin on St. Patrick's Day. As they were winging their way through the air, Harrigan turned to his friend Murphy and said, "Murphy, I'm going to fly upside down."
"Begorrah, Harrigan," shouted Murphy, "don't do that! To be sure, we'll fall out!"
"No, we won't," responded Harrigan.
"I'll still talk to you."

An Englishman stops Paddy for directions.
"Excuse me, pal, what's the quickest way to Dublin?"
Paddy says, "Are you on foot or in a car?"
"In the car," says the Englishman.
Paddy replies: "That's the quickest!"

Kerryman wants the carpenter to make him a box two inches deep, four inches wide and 50 feet long.
"I suppose it could be done... but why?"
"My neighbour moved away and forgot a few things.
"He asked me to send him his garden hose."

An Englishman, a Scotsman and a Kerryman are walking together when they encounter a slide that leads into a magic pool.
The Englishman decides to give it a try and shouts as he slides down: "Beer!" He lands in a pool of beer.
The Scotsman sees this and has a go himself. As he slides down, he cries out, "Whisky!" and lands in a pool of whisky.
The Kerryman thinks What a good idea, and it looks like fun.
As he slides down, he cries out, "Wheeeeee!"

Paddy was given a pair of water skis for Christmas and is still looking for a sloped lake to use them in.

Paddy was asked if he knew Ghandi's first name.
"Would it be Goosey Goosey?"

Paddy says you can tell the difference between a cow and a bull by trying to milk them both.
The one that smiles is the bull.

At a border checkpoint between Scotland and Ireland, five Scots in an Audi Quattro are stopped by Officer Paddy, who tells them: "It is illegal to put five people in that automobile. Quattro means four."
"Quattro is just the name," one of the astonished Scotsmen says. "This car is designed to carry five."
"You cannot pull that one on me," says Officer Paddy. "Quattro means four, there are five of you and you're all breaking the law.
The Scot replies angrily, "You idiot! Call over your supervisor! I want to speak to someone with more intelligence!"
"Sorry," responds Officer Paddy. "Murphy is busy with two guys in a Fiat Uno."

Paddy goes for a job at a chemical factory. "Do you know about chemicals?" he is asked.
 "For instance, can you tell me what nitrate is?"
"I'm hoping it'll be time and a half."

A kamikaze pilot from Kerry flew 3 missions.

The Kerryman who tried to row the Atlantic single-handed kept going round and round in circles.

Paddy went to the doctor and was told to give a urine sample.
"What's a urine sample?" he asked.
The doctor said, "Go piss in a bottle."
Retorted Paddy: "Go shit in your hat."

Paddy was charged with murder and acquitted by the skin of his teeth.
Afterwards, he told his lawyer that he could have proved he was innocent because he was in jail at the time of the murder.
"Why on earth didn't you tell that to the court?'
Said Paddy: "I thought that it might prejudice the court against me."

Paddy the pilot, asked for his height and position, said, "Six foot two and sitting in the front."

In a graveyard in Kerry: You may not pick flowers from any grave but your own.

One day three fellows walked into a pub together. One was from Belfast, one from Mayo and one from Kerry. They each bought a pint of Guinness. Just as they were about to take the first swallow, three flies landed in their pints, caught in the thick foam.
The Belfast fellow pushed his pint away in disgust.
The fellow from County Mayo continued drinking as if nothing had happened.
The Kerryman picked the fly out of his drink, held it over the beer, yelling: "SPIT IT OUT! SPIT IT OUT! SPIT IT OUT!"

A Kerryman asked where the Andes are, replied, "At the end of me armies."

Collective noun for a group of Kerrymen: a thicket.

A Kerryman is asked to sing a song.
"Ten green bottles, hanging on a wall, ten green bottles hanging on a wall...And if one green bottle should accidentally fall, there'll be... errr... um ...Oh, Danny Boy..."

When Paddy had to be buried at sea, four of his mates drowned trying to dig the hole.

Kerryman asked to fetch a wheelbarrow comes back wheeling one wheelbarrow inside another wheelbarrow.
 "Well, you didn't expect me to carry it, did you?" he explains.

Paddy thought that Sherlock Holmes was a block of flats.

Seamus says to Paddy, "It says here in the paper that during your whole life, you only use one-third of your brain."
Says Paddy: "What happens to the other third?"

What do you call a Kerryman with half a brain?
Gifted.

Paddy thought Johnny Cash was change from a condom machine.

He also thought Moby Dick was a venereal disease.

A woman drove Paddy to drink...and he didn't even have the decency to thank her.

Paddy is suing the bakery for unauthorized use of his signature on hot cross buns.

In County Kerry, one constable was promoted to sergeant from a class of 200. Each constable was asked only one question: How much is six times seven? The one who got promoted gave the answer Of forty-three.
He was the closest.

Kerryman on a building site had his ear knocked off by a falling brick. The ear was found by someone else.
"Is this yours?" he was asked.
"No, sir. Mine had a pencil behind it."

Paddy thought Pontius Pilate worked for Aer Lingus.

Four Kerrymen in a circle were arrested for smoking pot. Police said later that they had smashed a dope ring.

Paddy says: take my advice, I never use it.

Paddy and Murphy were flying together to Dublin when the captain spoke over the intercom:

"Sorry, ladies and gentlemen, but one of the engines just stopped. Don't worry, but we will be about half an hour late getting to Dublin."

Paddy and Murphy looked at each other but said nothing.

A little later, the intercom crackled again and the captain said,

"Sorry, ladies and gentlemen, but the second engine has just stopped. Nothing to worry about, but we will now be an hour late getting to Dublin airport."

Murphy and Paddy looked at each other but said nothing.

A bit later still, again the intercom came to life.

"Sorry, ladies and gentlemen, but a third engine has just given out. Nothing to worry about, but we will now be about four hours late into Dublin."

Paddy looked at Murphy and said, "Christ, if the fourth engine goes, we'll be up here forever!"

Kevin from Kerry goes into the neighborhood chemist, reaches into his pocket and takes out an Irish whisky bottle and a teaspoon. He pours out a teaspoonful and offers it to the chemist.

"Would you taste this for me, please?"

The chemist takes the teaspoon, puts in in his mouth, swills the liquid around and swallows it.

"Does that taste sweet to you?" asks Kevin.

"No, not at all," says the chemist.

"Oh that's a relief," says Kevin. "The doctor told me to come here and get my urine tested for sugar."

Two sweating Irishmen on a tandem bicycle at last reached the top of a steep hill.

"That was a stiff climb, Paddy," says one.

"That it was," says Paddy. "And if I hadn't kept the brake on, we'd have gone backwards, to be sure."

Paddy's boss noticed that his password was MARYMARTHABRIDGETBRIDEYNORABRENDA

"Why such a long password?" he asked.

"Because it says the password has to be at least six characters long."

[200]

Paddy was traveling with an Englishman and Scotsman in the Australian outback when the camper van broke down. They had to leave the van while they looked for help. Each could take only one thing from the van.
The Englishman took water to keep from becoming dehydrated.
The Scot took food for energy.
Paddy Irishman took the door.
They ask him: "Paddy, why did you take the door? It's very heavy."
Says Paddy: "But if I get too hot, I can roll down the window."

Irishman on a building site says, "What's a cubic foot, Paddy?"
Paddy says, "I don't know; but claim for it anyway."

Kerryman who drove the Kyalami 9-hour race had 32 pit stops: one for petrol and 31 to ask the way.

A Kerryman who found some milk bottles in a hedgerow thought he had discovered a cow's nest.

Paddy took a class in mythology. On a test, one question was what was half man and half beast.
Paddy's answer: Buffalo Bill.

What did Paddy do when he heard that 90% of all accidents happen in the home?
He moved.

Why can't Paddy make jello?
He can't figure out how to get 2 cups of water into that little paper packet.

Two Kerryman tourists in Florida drove hundreds of miles to see Disneyworld.
As they got on the last stretch of highway, they saw a sign saying DISNEYWORLD LEFT.
After a moment, the Kerryman driver said, "Oh, well!" and turned around to go back to their hotel.

When asked what's the capitol of Ireland, Paddy said, "Oh, that's easy! I!"

Paddy stared at the orange juice can for over an hour, because it said "Concentrate."

Two Kerrymen, Kearney and Riordan, were looking at a mail order catalog and admiring the models.

Says Kearney, "Aren't these girls lovely, now?

"Indeed," agrees Riordan. "And look at the price."

Kearney says, with wide eyes, "Begorrah, they are pretty cheap. At this price, I'm buying meself one."

Riordan pats his friend on the back. "Good idea. You order one and, if she's as good as she looks, I'll order one for meself."

Three weeks go by. Kearney says to Riordan: "Did you ever get that girl you ordered from the catalog?"

"No," says Riordan with a grin.

"But it shouldn't be long now.

"She sent all her clothes yesterday."

To a Kerrywoman, what's long and hard?
Fourth grade.

What's five miles long and has an IQ of 50?
A parade in County Kerry.

Why did Paddy turn down an elevator operator job?
He didn't know the route.

Paddy finally went to visit relatives in Boston; he'd never been out of Ireland before. He wrote his brother Seamus a letter:
"Seamus, Boston is an amazin' city. It's glass outhouses they got here, and it's telephones they put in 'em!"

What do you call an Irish spider?
Paddy Long Legs

Paddy went to night school to learn how to read in the dark.

Did you hear about the Kerryman who was stranded for an hour when the escalator broke down?

Paddy took his car to the mechanic who told him he needed a new muffler.
Paddy went right home and asked his wife to knit him one.

A Kerry surgeon was the first to separate a Siamese cat.

A tall Kerryman was holding up a telephone pole while a smaller man sat on his shoulders with a tape measure.
"Wouldn't it be easier to measure," asked a passerby, "if you laid the pole down?"
The tall fellow said, "We already know its length."
The little guy added, "And now we want to know its height."

Paddy always sleeps with a gun under his pillow. Hearing a noise at the foot of the bed, and being half asleep, he shot off his big toe. Said Paddy, "Thanks be I wasn't sleeping at the other end of the bed. I'd have blown my head off."

Paddy walks into a train station and presents himself at the ticket window.
"I'd like a return ticket."
"Where to, sir?"
"Why...here, of course!"

How do you make a Kerryman eyes light up?
Shine a flashlight in his ear.

Paddy went to New York City and first thing
he did was order a pizza.
The counter man asked should he cut it into
six pieces or twelve?
"Oh, six," says Paddy. "I could never eat
twelve."

He was offered Cheerios for breakfast at the
diner but wouldn't eat them. He thought
they were donut seeds.

Paddy's waitress at the diner was quite
buxom. He read her name tag and said,
"Debbie. That's a right grand name. What
d'ye call the other one?"

Men say the first thing they notice about a
woman is her eyes.
Women say the first thing they notice about
men is how they lie.

What does a Kerryman call true love?
An erection.

Paddy's wife says: I'm not one to repeat gossip, so listen very carefully, now.

Did you hear about the new County Kerry three million Euro lottery?
The winner gets three Euros a year for a million years.

Paddy goes to the doctor complaining of a sore leg. The doctor watches his limp and examines the leg carefully, gets tests done and asks Paddy to come back in two days. When Paddy comes back, the doctor says, "Paddy, we can find nothing wrong with your leg. I think it's a matter of getting older, that's all."
"Sorry to disagree, but that cannot be," says Paddy. "My other leg is just fine and it's exactly the same age as this one."

A Kerryman was suffering from sharp pains in his side. The doctor examined him and said, "You have acute appendicitis."
"Bejeezus, doctor," says Kerryman,
"I came here to get help, not a stupid compliment!"

Paddy goes to the local pub, buys a whisky and notices a peel-off prize sticker on the side of the glass. After pulling it off, he yells, "I won a caravan! I won a caravan, a nice big American one!"
The bartender shakes his head. "No, man, that's impossible. The biggest prize we give is a small telly."
"Look for yourself," says Paddy and hands the prize ticket to the bartender.
It says WIN A BAGEL.

What does Paddy say when you ask if his car blinker is working?
Yes. No. Yes. No. Yes. No. Yes. No. Yes, No.

Three Kerrymen are walking through a field when they come across a set of tracks.
The first Kerryman says, "Could be bird tracks."
Second Kerryman goes to look and says, "No, I think these are deer tracks."
The third Kerryman says, "Let me take a look."
He examines the tracks and gets run over by the train.

Paddy asked someone for the time and they told him it was 4:45. Paddy said:
"You know, this is very strange. I've been asking that question all day and every time I get a different answer."

Paddy finds a sandwich with two wires sticking out of it. He phones the police and says, I've just found a sandwich that looks like a bomb."
 "Is it tickin'?"
"No, I t'ink it's beef."

Two Kerrymen meet at the Galway races.
The first one whispers,
"Do you want the winner of the next race?"
"No thanks," says the second one.
"I've only got a small yard."

A Kerryman visiting London was treated very kindly by a Sikh bus driver.
When he got off at his stop, he said,
"Thanks very much, sir, and I hope your head gets better very soon."

On a plane bound for New York, the flight attendant approached Fergus from Kerry, who was sitting in a first-class seat with an economy ticket. "I'm afraid you'll have to move, sir. This is first class and you can't sit here," he said.

"I'm Fergus McGuinness, my family is first class in County Kerry, I'm going to New York, and I'm not moving."

The attendant calls on the co-pilot to speak with him. Says the co-pilot, "This is first-class and you don't have the proper ticket, sir. You'll have to move." But there's no moving this man.

The pilot is told the story and he says, "I'm married to a lass from Kerry and I know how to handle them."

He comes out and whispers in McGuiness's ear. "Ah, well, and why didn't you say so?" says McGuinness, and he moves.

Explains the pilot: I told him first class is not going to New York."

Paddy drove his new car over the cliff because he wanted to test the air brakes.

A coach full of Kerrymen is on a Mystery Tour and the passengers decide to run a sweepstakes to guess where they're going. The driver won 52 euros!

Paddy and Murphy are walking down a country road at night when Murphy falls into a deep hole.
He can't get out and what's more, he thinks he's broken his ankle.
"Paddy," he yells, "Call me an ambulance!"
Paddy begins to jump up and down, yelling: "Murphy's an ambulance! Murphy's an ambulance!"

Paddy and Thaddy are on a cruise together.
Thaddy says: "It's awfully quiet on this ship tonight."
"That's because everyone will be watching the band," says Paddy.
"What band? There's not a band playing tonight," says Thaddy.
Paddy says, "I definitely heard a fellow on the loudspeaker say 'a band on ship.'"

Paddy thinks '11' ought be called onety-one

A Kerryman was attacked by a robber and put up a spirited fight before giving up his purse which contained 50 cents.
"You put up such a struggle, just for 50 cents?" said the robber.
"No, I thought you were after the 50 euros I've got hidden in my left shoe."

Paddy says to his mate: "Don't come down that ladder. I've taken it away."

Did you hear that Paddy's library was burned down? Both books were destroyed, and worse still, one hadn't been coloured in yet.

Paddy went to insure his car and paid 20 euros to have it insured against fire.
"For 20 euros more, sir," said the agent, "you can insure it against theft also."
"That would be a waste of money," said Paddy.
"Who would want to steal a burning car?"

How do you know you're in Kerry? You see signs on the churches saying CLOSED ON SUNDAY.

Two Kerrymen were passing by a nudist colony. They decided to peep in over the wall and see what was going on inside. It was a very tall wall so one Kerryman stood on the other's shoulders.
"Are there both men and women there?" asked the man on the bottom.
"I can't tell," said the other. "They don't have any clothes on."

What do you call a Kerryman under a wheelbarrow?
A mechanic.
What do you call a Kerryman under a wheelbarrow with a cigarette in his mouth?
A welder.

Paddy wrote the following letter to the editor of a newspaper:
"Dear Sir, Last week I lost my gold pocket watch, so yesterday I put an ad in your LOST AND FOUND columns.
"Last night, I found my watch in the trousers of my other suit. God bless your newspaper!"

A Kerryman got a job as a lumberjack, but try as he might, he couldn't meet his quota of 50 trees a day.

Then he saw a notice in a shop window for chainsaws "guaranteed to fell 60 trees a day." Well, that looked good to him, so he bought one.

Still, the best he could manage was 40 trees a day.

He took the chainsaw back to the shop and complained that there must be something wrong with it.

"Let me take a look at it," said the clerk. He took the chainsaw and switched it on.

Said the Kerryman, "What's that noise?"

You don't get ice in your drinks in Kerry because the man with the recipe emigrated.

.

A Kerryman and a Kilkenny man are walking down a country road together.

The Kilkenny man says,

"Jaysus, isn't that a lovely view of the forest!"

Kerryman says, "Where? I can't see anything with all those trees in the way."

[214]

Paddy takes his goldfish to the vet. The vet watches the fish swimming and says, "I don't see anything wrong."
 Says Paddy, "You haven't taken him out of the bowl yet."

Paddy and Danny were taking a stroll when Danny spotted a mirror in the road. He picked it up and looked at it.
"Begorrah, I know that fella!" he exclaimed. Paddy took the mirror from him and looked. "Of course you know him. That's me!"

Paddy had a brain transplant. The brain rejected him.

Paddy was in the hospital. He had a Kerry nurse who kept waking him to take his sleeping tablets.

A Kerryman who had come into some money went to the doctor with an injury to his leg. "That looks nasty," said the doctor. "I'll fix it but I'd better give you a local anesthetic." "Hang the expense!" said the Kerryman. "I'll have the imported one!"

A Kerryman was happy he had cheated Irish Rail. He bought a return ticket to Dublin and didn't go back!

Paddy saw a notice reading: "Man wanted for Robbery and Murder." He went in and applied for the job.

Why do Kerry dogs have flat faces?
From chasing parked cars.

What do you do if a Kerryman throws a pin at you?
Run like mad; he's probably got a grenade between his teeth!

Paddy damaged his health by drinking milk. The cow fell on him!

Paddy won a round-the-world cruise in a raffle. He refused to accept the prize. "I have no way of getting back," he said.

Hand-drawn sign on Dublin road work cone: YE'LL NEVER GET TO WORK ON TIME. HA HA HA PADDY

[216]

Kerryman is up in Dublin and calls into an electrical shop. He asks the clerk behind the counter, "How much for that TV?" The clerk says, "We don't serve Kerrymen in here." So the Kerryman leaves, puts on a hat and dark glasses and comes back. He asks the same question and the clerk gives him the same answer. Now he changes his clothes and puts on a wig, changing his appearance altogether. Once again he asks how much for the tv and once again, he's told "We don't serve Kerrymen in here."
Defeated, he turns to leave, then asks, "How in the world did ye know I'm a Kerryman?" Says the clerk: "That's a microwave!"

Two Dublin city fellas were setting up a new store, which wasn't nearly finished. They sat down for a rest and one bet the other that, any minute, some thick culchie was going to look in and ask what they're selling. Sure enough, a curious Kerryman walks in, looks around and says, "What are ye selling, lads?" One of the men says, "Assholes." "Assholes, is it?" says Kerryman. "Well, you're doing well, you've only two left."

Why couldn't Paddy write the number eleven?
He didn't know which 'one' came first.

Father Christmas, the tooth fairy, a leprechaun and a Kerryman are walking together when they spot 10 euros lying in the gutter. Who picks it up? None of them. There is no such thing as Father Christmas, the tooth fairy, or a leprechaun; and the Kerryman thought it was a gum wrapper.

Why are Paddy jokes so short?
So Kerrymen can remember them.

Why did Paddy stare at the can of frozen orange juice for two hours?
Because on the can, it said "CONCENTRATE."

The man from Clare says: How do you save a Kerryman from drowning?
You don't know? Good.
The Kerryman retorts: What's the difference between a Clareman and a bucket of fertilizer?
The bucket.

Ten Kerryman and a woman were hanging on a rope under a helicopter.
They decided one of them had to drop off if they were not all destined to die.
The woman made a very eloquent goodbye speech saying she would gladly be the one because, as a true Irishwoman, she was used to giving up everything for her husband and family.
 When she finished talking, all the Kerryman began to clap their hands.

Paddy goes into a flag shop in Dublin.
"Tell me," he says. "What colours are the Irish flag?" "Green, white, and orange."
"Alright, then. I'll have a green one."

Two Kerrymen were strolling along in the countryside.
"Would you look at that dead bird," said one.
The second Kerryman peered up at the sky.
"Where?" he said.

What's the thinnest book on record?
The Kerry Book of Knowledge.

A Kerryman was truly skint and needed money badly. He decided to kidnap a child and hold the kid for ransom.
He went to a neighborhood play area, grabbed the first kid he saw, took her behind a building, and said, "I've kidnapped you." He then wrote a note in big letters saying, "I have kidnapped your kid. Tomorrow morning, put 10,000 euros in a paper bag and leave it under the apple tree near the gate on the South side. Signed, a Kerryman."
Kerryman then pinned the note to the child's shirt and sent her home to show to her parents. The next morning, he came back and sure enough, a paper bag was sitting beneath the apple tree. Kerryman looked in the bag and found the money along with a note that said, "How could you do this to a fellow Kerryman?"

Paddy went into a pub. "A pint of less, please."
The bartender frowned. "What's Less?"
"No idea," said Paddy. "But my doctor says I got to start drinking it"

A Kerryman complained to his local council about the very large puddle in his back garden and asked them to do something about it. Next day, they sent him 3 ducks.

Paddy is walking down the street when about ten feet away, he sees a banana peel. "Oh, no," he groans. "Here we go again!"

A television news reporter in County Kerry was interviewing a man for making a brave citizen's arrest.
"The Garda couldn't do it and the fire brigade couldn't do it and even the priest couldn't do it. How in the world did you get the one-armed cat burglar out of the tree?"
"Oh, it was easy," said the Kerryman.
"I waved to him."

Did you hear about the Kerry girl who had to give up her cello lessons?
The cello was too heavy and it really hurt her neck when she tucked it under her chin.

Few Irishwomen admit their age.
Few Irishmen act it.

O'Hara's wife couldn't help but notice that her husband was out in the back garden, leaning over the neighbour's fence shouting, "Green side up! Green side up!"
Eventually, she called out to him, "Thaddy, what's going on?"
"It's Paddy next door. He's laying some new turf."

The Kerry girl spent the whole day at the library, studying for her blood test.

Paddy went to see the doctor.
"It's drink that's made you into the slovenly, drunken, incontinent, rude and violent person that you are," said the doctor.
"Oh thanks, Doc!" said Paddy, greatly relieved. "And here me wife always said it was me own fault."

Kerryman's barbeque was not the success he had hoped for.
The chicken, steaks and sausages were cooked to perfection.
But the beans just kept falling through the grating.

[222]

"Well, and what do you think?" asked the English cousin who was showing Paddy around Stonehenge.
"It might do," said Paddy,
"When they finally finish it."

"Have you seen my boots?" Kerryman asked his wife.
"No, I haven't," said his wife. "Are you sure you had them on when you took them off?"

On a trip to Dublin Paddy went into Boots to get his wife a gift. He decided a soap bar.
"Would you like it scented?" asked the clerk.
"No, I'll just take it home meself."

Nobody is saying she was a wee bit thick; but Mary O'Kerry is the only woman I ever knew who would smile through a thunder and lightning storm, thinking someone was taking her picture.

On a Kerry restaurant's double doors:
Left side: PLEASE USE THE OTHER DOOR.
Right side: THIS IS THE OTHER DOOR.

Paddy walks into the pub with a roll of tarmac under his arm. "A pint for me," he says, "And one more for the road."

Paddy didn't seem himself on Friday night when Murphy met him in the pub for a drink. "What's the matter, then, Paddy?" he asked. "I dunno," replied Paddy. "I keep seein' these spots before my eyes."
"Have ye seen a doctor?"
"No, just them spots."

Malone was in the hospital awaiting brain surgery. He asked to speak to the surgeon. "Well, doc, I've been speaking with the Tipperaryman in the next bed and he's being charged 1000 pounds less than I am...and it's the same brain surgery!"
"You're a Kerryman." "What's that got to do with it?" "For you, there's a search fee."

Paddy's wife worked in an art supply store and sold artists' canvas by the yard, either 36" or 48" wide. A customer asked for five yards. Paddy's wife asked, "What width?" Perplexed, the customer said, "Scissors?"

Paddy worked on a construction site in Kerry. His foreman was not known for his compassion. So when Paddy came in late for work one morning, all covered in bruises and bandages and limping a bit, the manager only asked what had kept him.
"I fell down the stairs," said Paddy.
Said Kerryman manager: "And that took a whole hour?"

A fella from Cork and a Kerryman were backpacking in Canada. They were happily hiking through the woods when a huge brown bear suddenly appeared in the clearing about 50 feet in front of them. When the bear spotted the two men, he began to lumber toward them.
Davy from Cork dropped his backpack, dug out a pair of runners and frantically began to put them on.
Wee Seamus from Kerry said, "What are you doin'? Runners won't help you outrun that bear!"
"I don't need to outrun the bear," said Davy. "I only need to outrun you."

O'Leary goes into a pub in Kerry and asks for a pint of Guinness.
"That'll be one euro, sir," says the barman.
"That seems a fair price," says O'Leary.
"And would you like a glass with that, sir?"

Two Kerrymen meet on the street.
"Poor Michael Hogan! Faith, I'm afraid he's doin' to die!" says the one.
"Shure, and why would he be dyin'?" asked the other.
"Ah, he's gotten so thin. You're thin enough, and I'm thin...but by my soul, Michael Hogan is thinner than both of us put together!"

One night, Paddy, pretty drunk, came home from the pub with a pig under his arm.
"You're not bringing that thing into the house," his wife screamed.
"Whyever not?"
"The smell, Paddy, the smell!!"
"Oh," said Paddy,
"I'm sure he'll get used to it in time."

Why do Kerrymen go around all the time in three's?
Well, one of them can usually read and one of them can usually write and the third just likes to hang around intellectuals.

Paddy was right pleased when he found a PARKING FINE notice on his car.
He thought the police were paying him a compliment.

Two Kerrymen are playing Trivial Pursuit. One of them rolls the dice and it lands on Science and Nature. Says the one. "Here's your question. If you're in a vacuum and someone calls your name, will you be able to hear it?" Kerryman gives it some thought. "Is it on or off?" he says finally.

The Kerryman was about to get on a bus with his pet crocodile. "Hey," said the conductor, "you can't bring a crocodile on my bus. What're you doing with it? You should take it to the zoo!"
"I did!" said Kerryman. "And now I'm taking him to the cinema."

[227]

Paddy was doing 90 mph down a motorway when the police stopped him.

He said he was going so fast because he had diarrhea and he wanted to get home before it was too late.

The police let him off, but warned him it was a very dangerous thing to do, even more dangerous than if he had been driving a car at the time.

Dylan went around to Paddy's house and found him in the living room strewn with boards and nails and doors and screws and other building materials.

"What's up, Paddy?" he asked.

"Oh, it's this self-assembly furniture I've just bought. It's rubbish," moaned Paddy.

"I've been watching it for three hours now and it still hasn't done a thing. If I have to wait any longer, I'm going to do it meself."

A boy had been chatting up a lovely Kerry lass all evening at the nightclub. It was going really well until he asked if he could see her home and she showed him a photo of her parents' house.

Archimedes, the well-known truth seeker
Jumping out of his bath, cried, "Eureka!"
He ran half a mile,
Wearing only a smile,
And became the world's very first streaker.

A famous theatrical actress
Played best in the role of malefactress.
Yet her home life was pure,
Except, be sure,
A scandal or two, just for practice.

A girl called Miss Fortune sighed, "Oh,
My name's a misfortune, I know.
Miss Takes's just as bad
And Miss Fitt is quite mad,
And that Miss B. Haviour must go!"

A longely old maid named Loretta
Sent herself an anonymous letter,
Quoting Ellis on sx,
And Eodipus Rex,
And exclaimed, "I already feel better!"

[229]

A Kerryman was driving from Tralee to Galway and his wife moaned at him the entire way.
She moaned at him when they left County Kerry, she moaned at him when he made a stop to pee, she moaned at him when they got to Galway.
She even moaned at him when he untied her from the roof rack.

A Kerryman coming from Clyde
In a funeral march was espied.
When asked, "Who is dead?"
He just giggled and said:
"I don't know. I just came for the ride."

Told they would have to wait 45 minutes to be seated at a restaurant, the elderly Kerryman said "I'm not sure we <u>have</u> 45 minutes." They were seated immediately.

KERRYMAN: Can you name three consecutive days without using Wednesday, Friday or Sunday?
PADDY: To be sure. Today, yesterday, and tomorrow.

THE CHURCH

THE BEST OF IRISH HUMOR

An Irishman was trying to learn golf and
having a terrible time of it. "I'd give just
about anything to get this right," he said.
The Devil appeared and said, "Anything?"
"Short of selling my soul, yes."
"How about giving up sex for the rest of
your life?"
"Done'" He finishes the game in rare good
form, and rumor of his deal spreads
throughout the clubhouse.
One of the members, a reporter, asks him,
"Sir, is it true you made a deal with the
Devil to become a great golfer?"'
"True enough."
And you gave up sex as your part of the
bargain?"
"True again."
And may I have your name, Sir?"
"Certainly. Father Michael Ryan."

Mother Superior called all her nuns together
and said, "I'm very sorry to have to tell you
this; but we seem to have a case of
gonorrhea in the convent."
"Thank God," said an elderly nun at the back
of the room. "I'm tired of Chardonnay."

[233]

Father O'Malley dies and is waiting in line to be greeted by St. Peter. He's right behind Murphy the cabbie.

St. Peter says to Murphy, "We have a lovely mansion with gardens and a pool for you." Then he says to the priest, "Ah, Father, we have a cozy little two-room cottage for you." Father O'Malley is stunned.

"Why do I get a tiny cottage and Murphy here, a mansion?"

St. Peter says, "Father, it's like this. When you preached, people slept.

"When Murphy drove his cab, people prayed."

One Sunday morning, the Priest saw little Sean staring up at the large plaque that hung in the church's foyer. The plaque was covered with names and small flags.

"Father Ryan," the boy asked, "What's this?"

"Well son, it's a memorial to all the young men and women who died in the service," the priest said.

Little Sean asked, with trepidation:

"Which service, 9.00 or 10:30?"

Sister Mary enters Flynn's liquor store and orders a bottle of Irish whiskey. Flynn frowns and asks, "You're a nun, why would you want a bottle of Irish whiskey?" Sister Mary says, "It's for Father Donovan, he's constipated."
Flynn nods and puts a bottle in a bag.
Later that night, Flynn sees Sister Mary drunk in an alley with the empty bottle at her side.
Flynn yells, "You said it was for Father Donovan's constipation!"
Sister Mary responds, "And so it is. When he sees me, he's gonna shit."

"Don't think you have time to repent!" shouted the priest in his sermon.
"Before the day is ended, someone in this parish will die!"
He heard laughter from the back.
"Why do you laugh?" he demanded.
"Why? Because I'm not a member of this parish!"

Thursday night potluck dinner at St. Brigit's. Prayer and meditation to follow.

A man flops down into a subway seat next to a priest. The man is in terrible disarray. His face is smeared with lipstick, his hair is mussed and a half-empty pint of gin is sticking out of his torn coat pocket. He opens a paper and begins reading.

After a few minutes, this man turns to the priest and asks, "Say, Father, what causes arthritis?" "Loose living, cheap wicked women; too much alcohol; and contempt for your fellow man," says the priest. "I'll be damned," mutters the man and returns to his newspaper.

The priest thinks about what he said and nudges the man. "I'm very sorry," he says. "I didn't mean to be so harsh. How long have you had arthritis?"

"Oh, I don't have it, Father.

"But it says here that the Pope does."

An Episcopal bishop takes a cab from JFK and asks to go to "Christ's Church." The cabbie takes him to St. Pat's. "This isn't right!" says the bishop.

Says the cabbie: "If He ain't here, yer Excellency, He just ain't in town."

Bridget Clancy goes up to Father O'Brien after his Sunday 10 o'clock Mass, and she's in tears.
He says, "So what's' bothering you Bridget?"
She says, "Oh Father, I've got terrible news. My husband passed away last night"
The Priest says, "Oh Bridget, that's awful. Tell me, did he have any last requests?"
"That he did, Father"
The Priest says, "What did he say, Bridget?"
She says, "'Please Bridget, Put down the gun.'"

Kevin Houlihan kept falling asleep during Mass. To wake him, his wife would poke him with her hat pin. This irked Kevin, and besides, it hurt. The priest was talking about the Immaculate Conception. Just as he asked the rhetorical question: "And how do we think Mary felt, to hear this glorious news?" Kevin began to snore and was poked hard. Waking, he shouted: "You poke that damn thing into me one more time, and I'll break it and shove it up your rear!!"
"Amen!" responded all the women in the congregation.

Two nuns, Sister Frances and Sister Helen are traveling through Transylvania in their car when they're stopped at a light. Suddenly, out of nowhere, a diminutive Dracula jumps onto the hood of the car and hisses at them through the windshield.
"Holy Mother!" shouts Sister Frances.
"Would you look at that! What shall we do?"
"Turn on the wipers. That should do it."
Sister Frances switches on the windshield wipers, knocking Dracula about; but he clings on and continues hissing at them.
"What shall we do now?"
"Switch on the windshield washer. I filled it up with holy water when we were at the Vatican." Dracula screams with pain but holds on.
"Now what?" demands Sister Frances.
"Show him your cross!"
"Now you're talkin'!" says Sister Frances, as she opens the window, leans out, and yells, "Get the f___ off our car!"

"Father, is it okay to have sex before receiving Communion?"
"Only if you don't block the aisle."

[238]

Eileen McDermott knelt in the confessional and said, "Father, I have committed the sin of vanity. I look in the mirror all the time. I even take a peek in the plate glass windows of stores as I pass by. And twice a day, I tell myself how beautiful I am."

The priest took a look through the peephole, and said, "My dear, I have good news. That isn't a sin at all...it's only a mistake."

Sister Mary Katherine entered the Monastery of Silence. She wasn't allowed to speak unless directed to do so by Brother Brian. After five years, Brother Brian said to her, "You may speak two words." "Hard Bed," said the nun. "We will get you a new bed." After another five years, Brother Brian said, "You may speak another two words, Sister." "Cold food," said Sister Mary Katherine; and the monk assured her it would be better in future.

After another five years, she was allowed to speak two words and said, "I quit."

"That's probably best," said Brother Brian, "You've done nothing but complain since you got here."

Two priests died at the same time and met St. Peter together at the Pearly Gates.
"I'd like to get you guys in now," said St. Peter, "but our computer's down. You'll have to go back to Earth for a few days, but you can't go back as humans. What'll it be then?"
The first priest said, "I've always wanted to be an eagle, soaring above the mountains."
"So be it," says St. Peter, and the eagle flies off.
The second priest mulls this over and says, "Will anything we'd be doing count against us?"
"No, as I told you, the computer's down."
"In that case, I've always longed to be a stud." "So be it," says the saint and the priest disappears.
After the computer is fixed, St. Peter is told to recall the two priests. "Will you have any trouble locating them?" he is asked.
"Well, the first one should be easy. He's somewhere over the Rockies, flying with the other eagles. But the other? That'll be more difficult. He's on a snow tire, somewhere in Minnesota."

Muldoon lived all alone with his dog. When the dog died, Muldoon went to the parish priest and asked, "Could ya be saying a mass for the poor creature?"
"Certainly not! "Tis not allowed in the Church. But there's some Baptists down the lane might do it."
"I'll ask them," said Muldoon. "Would a E5,000 donation be enough, d'you think?"
"Sweet Mary! Why did you not tell me the dog was Catholic!.

Branigan worked all his life in the local lumber yard and all that time he'd been stealing the wood and using it or selling it. At last his conscience began to bother him he went to confession to repent.
"Forgive me, Father, for I have sinned," he said. "It's been twenty years since my last confession. And I've been stealing wood from the lumber yard all those years."
"That's not good, my son," said the priest. "Can you make a Novena?"
Branigan said, "Father, if you have the plans, I've surely got the lumber."

Father Murphy walks into a pub in Donegal and says to the first man he sees. "Do you want to go to heaven?"

"That I do, Father."

The priest said, "Then leave the bar and stand over there against the wall."

He then walked up to another man. "Do you want to go to heaven?"

"Certainly, Father."

"Then step away and stand over against that wall."

Then Father Murphy came to Flanigan. "Do you want to go to heaven?" he said.

Flanigan said, "No, I don't, Father."

"I don't believe this," said the priest. "You mean to tell me when you die, you don't want to go to heaven?"

Flanigan said, "Oh when I die, yes. I thought you were getting a group together to go right now."

When a restaurant opened next to a chapel, it put out a sign saying "Open Sundays." The chapel reciprocated with its own message: "We are open on Sundays, too."

A nun gets on a Dublin bus late at night and sits behind the driver.

When the last passenger but her gets off, she tells the bus driver she just found out she's very ill and she would like to experience sex before she dies.

The bus driver agrees to accommodate her.

The nun says she cannot do it if he's married because that would be a sin.

The driver assures her that he is not married.

The nun says she must die a virgin so it has to be anal sex and the driver is quick to agree.

Since they are the only two people on the bus, the driver pulls into a large and deserted parking lot and they go to the back seat and take care of business.

When he resumed driving, the driver said, "I have a confession to make. I am married and have three children."

The nun replies: "That's okay. I have a confession, too.

"My name is Mike and I'm on my way to a costume party."

One fine day in Ireland, a man is out golfing and at the 16th hole, he tees up and hits away. Sadly, it goes into the woods, so he goes looking for his ball. And lying there is a teeny little guy in green with a big bump on his head and the golf ball beside him. The golfer proceeds to revive the poor little guy. Upon awaking, the little guy says, "Well, you got me fair and square. I'm a leprechaun and I'm obliged to grant you three wishes." The golfer says, "I can't take anything from you. I'm just glad you weren't badly hurt." And he walks away. The leprechaun thinks, There goes a nice fellow and he did catch me so I'll give him the three things I'd want: unlimited money, a great golf game, and a great sex life. A year goes by, and there's the same golfer on the same course at that 16th hole and once again he hits his ball into the rough. When he finds his ball, there's that same leprechaun. The golfer asks him how he's doing.
"I'm fine," says the leprechaun, "but might I ask how is your golf game?"
"It's great! I'm under par every time!"

Says the leprechaun, "I did that for you.
And might I ask after your finances?"
"Well, now that you ask, every time I put
my hand in my pocket, I come up with a
hundred dollar bill."
"I did that for you. And, how's your sex
life?"
The golfer blushes. "Once or twice a week,"
he says
"Is that ALL, such a young man? I don't
believe it!"
The golfer says, "Well, that's not bad for a
Catholic priest in a small parish."

CHURCH SIGNS

Trespassers will be baptized.

Don't wait for the hearse to take you to
church.

No God, No Peace – Know God, Know Peace

Come work for the Lord. The work is hard,
the hours are long and the pay is low. But
the retirement benefits are out of this world!

Sister Margaret had been a model nun all her life; but then she was called to her reward. As she approached the gates, St. Peter said, "Hold on, Sister Margaret. Not so fast!"

"But I've been good all my life, and dedicated to the work of the Lord! I cannot believe this!"

"Well," said St. Peter, "that's part of the problem. You've never learned right from wrong and to get into heaven, you must know the difference."

"What can I do?" I'll do anything!" pleaded the nun.

"I'm going to send you back to earth and I want you to smoke a cigarette. Call me when you are finished, and we'll discuss your situation."

The nun went to earth, smoked a strong cigarette and then called St. Peter, coughing and hacking. "St. Peter! I can hardly breathe, my mouth tastes terrible, my breath stinks, and it's no good!"

"Fine," said the saint. "You're getting a feel for right and wrong. Now go out tonight, drink some hard liquor and then call me."

Sister Margaret called after several belts of Jack Daniels. "St. Peter...I feel woozy ... that vile liquid burned my throat and nauseates me. It's all I can do to keep it down."
"Excellent, excellent. Now you are seeing the difference between right and wrong. Tonight, I want you to seek out a man and have sex with him and then call me again."
A week later, Sister Margaret called St. Peter and left a message: "Hello, Pete... it's Peggy. I'm going to be gone for a while!"

There was a monastery where every morning the head monk would chant "Good Mo-or-ning!" and the other monks would chant back, "Good mo-or-ning!"
Every evening, the head monk would chant, "Good eve-ening!" and all the other monks would chant back, "Good eve-ening!"
Well, one day a new monk arrived from Europe, all jet-lagged and tired, so confused that when the head monk chanted, "Good mo-or-ning!" he answered, "Good eve-ening!"
And the head monk said,
"Someone chanted eve-en-ning!"

[247]

The new priest at his first mass was so nervous, he asked Father Murphy, the old priest what he should do. "Well, I take me a wee bit o' whisky to calm me nerves," said Father Murphy. The next Sunday, the new priest took a drink and talked up a storm. Upon returning to his office after Mass, he found the following note tacked to his door.

.A few sips of whisky. Not the entire bottle.

.There are 10 commandments, not 12.

.There are 12 disciples, not ten.

.Jesus was consecrated, not constipated.

.Jacob wagered his donkey, he did not bet his ass.

.We do not refer to Jesus Christ as the late J.C.

.The Irish Father, Son and Holy Ghost are not referred to as Senior, Junior and the Spook.

.David slew Goliath, he did not kick the shit out of him.

.You do not refer to the Cross as the Big T.

. Next Sunday there will be a taffy-pulling contest at St. Patrick's, not a Patrick-pulling contest at St. Taffy's.

.The recommended grace before a meal is not "Rub a dub dub, thanks for the grub, yea God!"

In the Middle Ages, St Brendan was supervising the good monks who were slavishly copying all the church manuscripts, with all the rules.
Suddenly, he gave out a horrible howl of agony.
"Brothers!" he cried. "The word is 'CELEBRATE!'"

Two nuns are walking down an alley at night. Two guys jump them and start raping them. The first nun looks to heaven, and prays: "Forgive them, Father, for they know not what they are doing."
The other says, "This one does!"

On their way to get married, a young Catholic couple was involved in a total car smashup.

They soon found themselves sitting outside the pearly gates, waiting for St. Peter to process them into Heaven. While waiting, they began to wonder: could they possibly get married in Heaven?

When St. Peter arrived, they asked him. St. Peter said, "I don't really know. It's the first time I've ever been asked that question. Let me go find out."

The couple sat and waited and waited … and waited.

Several months went by.

While they waited, they discussed the pros and cons of the idea. If they could get married in Heaven, what was the eternal prospect of it all? What if it didn't work? Would we be stuck in Heaven together for all Eternity?

St. Peter finally returned, looking somewhat bedraggled.

"Yes," he informed them. "You can get married in Heaven."

"Oh, that's wonderful," said the woman.

"But... we were just wondering... What if things don't work out? Could we also get a divorce in Heaven?"

St. Peter's face turned red with frustration. He slammed his clipboard onto the ground.

"What's wrong?" asked the frightened woman.

"What's wrong?? COME ON!!!" St. Peter shouted.

"It took me three months to find a priest up here!

"Do you have any idea how long it'll take to find a lawyer?"

It's reported that three Latin nations,
Have monopolized canonisations.
It seems rather quaint
That a non-Latin saint
Get a halo—but with limitations.

Call us comrades or amigos or mates,
Or even buddies, the term in the States;
Secure in the knowledge
We belong to the college
With the Pope we're to have tete-a-tetes.

There was a young Bishop from Spain
Who would not from speaking refrain;
But he went much too fast
From the first to the last,
The rest found his Latin a strain.

We all admit that the deacon
Could shine in the Church like a beacon.
"But...with a celibate's vows,
Or as a man with a spouse?"
It the question whose answer we're seekin'.

The Limerick's inferior, they say
To the poetry of Shelley or Gray.
But the Bishop of "X,"
Without wishing to vex,
Composes at least one a day.

Bishop Herras has made the proposal
That Coadjutors are ripe for disposal
For it's hardly humane
So long to remain
Without definite hope of espousal.

[252]

Oh, Lord, I can prove intellectual,
A doctor profoundly effectual,
Whose teachings are sure
If YOU keep me pure
With thoughts that are solely asexual.

This limerick's for purging my sin,
Ousting lust and desire from within,
Which leaves oodles of space
For agape and grace,
Plus humility virtue, and gin.

If Bibles for porn have been traded
You might think that horribly jaded.
Holy word or just prose?
No one really knows,
So it's hard to tell when they're degraded.

Religion, though thought an adviser
Instead is much more like a miser.
Holding onto the Scripture
Despite the wrong picture,
It's older, but not any wiser.

[253]

Dolly Parton and Queen Elizabeth die on the same day; and they both go before St. Peter to find out if they'll be admitted to Heaven. Unfortunately, there's only one space left that day, so St. Peter must decide which of them gets in.

St. Peter asks Dolly Parton is there's some particular reason she should get in.

Dolly takes off her shirt and says, "People tell me these are the most perfect breasts in the world. Perhaps all the angels would be happy to see them every day for Eternity."

St. Peter thanks her and asks Her Majesty the same question.

The Queen takes a bottle of Perrier out of her purse, shakes it up, and gargles. Then she spits into a toilet and pulls the lever.

St. Peter chuckles and says, "Very well, Your Majesty, you may go in now."

Dolly is outraged and demands, "What was THAT about?" "Sorry, Dolly," says St. Peter. "But, even in Heaven, a royal flush beats a pair—no matter how big they are."

Sign in front of a church: Free trip to heaven! Details inside!

[254]

The elderly Irish priest was becoming upset at how often he heard the word "adultery" in the confessional. He gently suggested to his congregation that they use the word "fallen" instead; he would know what they were talking about and the penances would remain the same. When he died, a new priest came to take over the parish.
After a week or two, the new priest went to have a talk with the town's mayor. "Sure, and you've got to do something about the town's sidewalks and alleyways, Mayor," he said. "I've never heard of so many people falling. It's a menace."
The mayor figured out what the priest was referring to and let out a roar of laughter. Indignant, the priest said, "You wouldn't think it was so funny if I told you your own wife has fallen twice this past week!"

After many lapsed years, Patrick goes into a confessional. He finds Guiness on tap, a full bar and a fine array of cigars.
"The Church has surely changed," he thinks. Then the priest comes in. "Get out, you moron," he says. "You're on my side."

[255]

A priest and a rabbi found themselves in the same compartment on the train for Belfast. After a while, the priest said, "I understand that, in your religion, you're not supposed to eat pork. Have you actually ever tasted it?" The rabbi said, "To tell the truth, yes I have, on the odd occasion. But, tell me...I know you're supposed to be celibate, but..."
The priest replied, "Yes, I know what you're going to ask. I have succumbed, just once or twice." They sat in silence for a short time. Then, the rabbi peered around his newspaper and said, "Beats the hell out of a ham sandwich, don't you think?"

When my older brother, Shay, was very young, he always walked up to the church altar with our mother when she took Communion.
On one occasion, he tugged at her arm and asked, "What does the priest say when he gives you the bread?" She whispered something in his ear.
Imagine his shock years later when he learned the priest does not say, "Be quiet until you get back to your seat."

Two Dublin lads were out carousing with their girlfriends. One felt guilty and decided he should stop at the nearby church and confess.

In the confession booth, he said, "Forgive me, Father, for I have sinned. I have been fornicating all the weekend. Please forgive me."

"And who is this loose lady?" asked the priest.

"Oh, I couldn't tell you her name, that wouldn't be fair," said the young man.

"Well, I cannot forgive until I know who she is. Was it Molly O'Grady?"

"No."

"Rosie Kelly?"

"No."

"Was it that red-headed wench Tessie O'Malley?"

""I cannot tell you, Father."

"Then you'll not be forgiven. Off with you."

When the lad met his friend outside the church, the friend asked, "So did you find forgiveness?"

"No," he said, "But I picked up three good prospects."

God is tired, really worn out. He goes to St. Peter. "I need a vacation. Got any suggestions?"

St. Peter says, "How about Jupiter? It's nice and warm on that planet this time of year."

God shakes his head. "No, I don't think so. Too much gravity. You know how that hurts my back."

St. Peter reflects. "How about Mercury?"

"Too hot and humid! No, I don't think so."

St. Peter and God sit together and think. Finally, St. Peter says, "How about Earth for a couple of millennia?"

"Are you kidding?" says God. Two thousand years ago, I went there, had a brief affair with a Jewish girl, and they're still going on and on about it!"

And God created Woman and she had three breasts. She complained to God. "I'm not meant to have litters. I need only two breasts." "Thou sayest wisely," said God. Poof! the extra breast was in his hand. "What will you do with that worthless boob?" asked woman.

And so it was that God created Man.

Three nuns who had recently died were on their way to heaven. At the gates, they were met by St. Peter. They noticed that around the gates were bells and lights.

St. Peter stopped them and explained that each of them would have to answer a question before they could enter through the gates of heaven.

St. Peter: What were the names of the first two people in the Garden of Eden

1st nun: Adam and Eve.

The lights flashed and the bells rang out and the gates opened wide and in she went.

St. Peter: Next question. What did Adam eat from the forbidden Tree of Knowledge?

2nd nun: An apple.

The lights flashed again, the bells rang, the gates opened and in went the nun.

St. Peter: What were the first words Eve said to Adam?

The 3rd nun wrinkled her brow and thought hard. She couldn't remember ever seeing those words in the Bible. "Mmmm," she said, "That's a hard one."

The lights flashed, the bells rang, the gates opened, and in she went.

Brothers Sean and Seamus Riordan were the richest men in town –and mean, to boot.

They swindled the church out of its property, foreclosed on widows and orphans...and that was just for starters.

Finally, Seamus caught a cold and it turned into pneumonia and suddenly, he was dead. Sean paid a visit to the priest at St. Brigit's.

"Father," he said to the priest, "I want to make sure that the Riordan name stays bright and shining. You'll be giving the eulogy for my brother Seamus and I want you to say: "'Seamus Riordan was truly a saint.'"

"I'll be damned if I will!" retorted the priest.

"Well, now, and I'm sure you <u>will</u> say those words. I own the mortgage on the parish school and if you don't say them, I'll foreclose before you can say a Hail Mary."

The priest was over a barrel. And then he had an idea.

"And if I say those words, you'll sign over the note free and clear?"

"Done," cackled Sean, rubbing his hands together."All right, then."

He can hardly wait for the funeral service.

Next, morning, at the funeral, the priest began the eulogy. "Seamus Riordan was a spiteful, mean-spirited, evil, penurious, lying, cheating, arrogant and hateful excuse for a human being.
But compared to his brother, he was truly a saint."

Pat and Mike are sitting in a pub drinking beer and watching the brothel across the road. They see a Rabbi go up to the front door, look around furtively, and duck inside.
"Will you look at that," says Pat. "What's our world coming to when a man of the cloth goes to a place like that!"
A short time later, the local Protestant minister walks up to the front door and quietly slides inside.
"D'you believe that?" exclaims Mike. "Why, 'tis no wonder our young folks are so confused, what with the example clergymen set for them!"
An hour later, they watched as a Catholic priest quickly entered the house.
"What a pity!" says Pat.
"One of the lasses must be very ill!"

[261]

Two leprechauns visited the Mother Superior
of a convent: They asked her, "Do you have
any nuns here who are of the little people?
Midgets?" "No, we do not." "Do you know
of any such nun anywhere in Ireland?" "No,
I do not." One leprechaun said to the other,
"You see? It's just as I've been telling you.
You've fallen in love with a penguin!"

There was a young monk from Siberia
Whose morals were very inferior.
He did to a nun
What he should not have done
And now she's a Mother Superior.

A divine by the name of O'Finners
Held classes each evening for sinners.
They were sectioned and graded
So the very degraded
Would not be held back by beginners.

There was a young lady called Alice
Who peed in a Catholic chalice.
The padre agreed
It was done out of need
And not out of Protestant malice.

Three men arrived at the pearly gates together and were met by St. Peter. It was Christmas Eve and the Saint said, "You must each possess something that symbolizes Christmas to get into heaven."

The first man looked through his pockets and pulled out a lighter. He flicked it on, saying "It represents a candle."

He was allowed to pass.

The second man searched though his pockets and pulled out a set of keys. He shook them together and said, "These are bells."

He, too, was allowed to pass through the pearly gates.

The third man began searching desperately through his pockets. Finally, he pulled out a pair of lacy women's panties.

St. Peter raised an eyebrow and asked, "Just what do those symbolize?"

The man replied, "They are Carol's."

A young priest asks a nun if he can walk her to her convent. "Just this once, yes," she says. At the convent gate, he asks for a kiss. "Okay, but don't get into the habit."

A very old person of Fratton
Would sit through Mass with his hat on
"When I wake up," he said
"With my hat on my head,
"I shall know that it hasn't been sat on."

A handsome young monk in a wood
Told a girl she should cling to the good.
She obeyed him but gladly,
He repulsed her, but sadly,
And said she had misunderstood.

Elderly Father Flanagan invited young Father Finn, fresh from the seminary, for dinner. While they dined, Father Finn couldn't help but notice how very attractive and shapely the housekeeper was.

He wondered if perhaps there might be more than met the eye to the relationship between elderly priest and young housekeeper.

Father Flanagan noticed his guest staring and said, "I assure you that my relationship with Sheila is strictly professional."

About a week later, Sheila came to the priest and said, "Ever since Father Finn came to dinner, I cannot find our beautiful silver ladle. I cannot believe that he would take it."

The old priest wrote a note to the younger, saying how much he had enjoyed their visit. "On another matter...we had a beautiful silver ladle which was a gift from a parishioner. The ladle has come up missing. Now I'm not saying that you *did* take a ladle from my house or that you *did not*.

"But the fact remains that it has been missing since you were here for dinner." Several days later, a letter from Father Finn was delivered.

"Dear Father Flanagan,

I enjoyed the dinner and our visit. On the matter of the silver ladle, now, I'm not saying that you *do not* sleep with your housekeeper; nor am I saying that you *do* sleep with her.

"But the fact remains that if you were sleeping in your own bed, you would have found the gravy ladle by now."

A nun is undressing for her bath and while she's standing naked, there's a knock at her door.

"Who is it?" she calls.

"The blind man," comes the answer.

The nun thinks how interesting it will be to be naked while a blind man is in the room, and him not knowing. She lets him in.

He walks in, carrying a long wrapped package.

Then he looks straight at her and says, "Coooor, m'dear, and can I interest you in some of me blinds?"

Halfway through Mass, the priest suddenly asked: "Will all the good people who would like to go to Heaven please stand up." The whole congregation stood. "That's very nice," said the priest. "You may all sit down now." Then, he said, "And if there's anyone here would like to go to Hell, will you please stand up." Everyone remained seated. "Nobody?" Whereupon Connery in the back pew stood. "Connery," said the priest, "I'm surprised." Said Connery, "Well, I didn't like to see you standing there all by yourself."

Why worry? In the end, there are only two
things to worry about: either you are well
or you are sick.
When you are well, there's nothing to worry
about.
But if you're sick, there are only two things
to worry about: whether you will get well or
you will die.
If you get well, there's nothing to worry
about.
But if you die, there are only two things to
worry about: either you will go to heaven or
you will go to Hell.
If you go to heaven, there's nothing to worry
about.
But if you go to Hell, you'll be so damn busy
shaking hands with all your friends, you
won't have time to worry.
So, why worry?

Notice in a church parking lot:
Warning! Trespassers will be baptized.

Out in the front of the church:
In the dark? Follow the Son.

A man is driving along a deserted stretch of road in Galway, when he notices a sign saying SISTERS OF MERCY HOUSE OF PROSTITUTION. Sure it was his imagination, he drives on. Around the next bend is another sign. SISTERS OF MERCY HOUSE OF PROSTITUTION, NEXT RIGHT. This is too good to miss, he thinks, and pulls into the drive. There's a small stone building off to the side with a small sign saying Sisters of Mercy. He rings the bell, which is answered by a nun in a long black habit. "What can I do for ye, my son?" He tells her he saw the signs along the road and, well, um... "Follow me," she says. They stop at a big wooden door. "Knock three times," she tells him; and he does so. Another nun holding a large tin cup answers the door. "Please place $50 in the cup, then go through the door at the end of this hallway." Eagerly, he follows her instructions and closes the door behind him. He hears the door lock and sees that he is in the parking lot, facing another small sign. GO IN PEACE. YOU HAVE JUST BEEN SCREWED BY THE SISTERS OF MERCY.

Mother Superior: Sister Maria, if you walk through town at night and you're accosted by a man with bad intentions, what do you think you would do??

Sister Maria: I would lift my habit, Mother.

Mother Superior: I am shocked! And what would you do next?

Sister Maria: I would tell him to drop his trousers.

Mother Superior: I cannot believe this! And what then, Sister Maria?

Sister Maria: I would run away. A nun with her skirts up can go a lot faster than a man with his pants down.

A group of people are touring the White House in Washington, D.C. As the tour ends, they are all waiting in line to sign the visitors' register.

A group of Irish nuns are in line to sign the book, followed by a Jewish family with their young son, Sheldon.

As the line inches closer to the registry, young Sheldon loses patience and jumps the line. His mother admonishes him:

"Wait 'til the nuns sign, Shelly!"

[269]

A nun is driving the convent's car through a long stretch of countryside near Galway. Suddenly the car stops and she sees that the petrol indicator is on Empty.
She had noticed a filling station half a mile back, so she sets out to ask them for some petrol. There is no canister in the car; but in the boot, she finds a hospital chamber pot. She walks back to the station and the attendant puts petrol into the chamber pot and she walks back to the car.
As she is pouring the petrol into the tank, a car slows down to see what she is doing. From the driver's window, she hears:
"Sister, how I would like to have as much faith as you do!"

Sister Mary Jane was walking to the convent when a man jumped out of the bushes and had his way with her.
When he had finished, he said, "What will you tell the Holy Father about this when you confess?"
"The truth, of course. A man jumped out of the bushes and raped me twice...
Unless you're too tired."

Four Irish priests were on a long train trip. After looking at the scenery for a while, one said, "You know, we don't really know each other. I suggest each of us confess one sin. And, since I'm the one suggested it, I'll go first.

"It's the drink with me. I can control it for the most part but once a year I take off my collar and go on a bender."

The second priest says, "Once a year, I take money out of the poor box and go to the races and gamble."

The third priest hesitates, then says, "Oh, well, I might as well confess. Once a year, I dress in normal clothes and spend a week in the red-light district."

The fourth priest says nothing, a strange look on his face.

The first one says, "Come now, man, we've all told our tales. It's your turn."

The fourth priest hesitates, looks at the others, and says,

 "Well, fellas, I'm an inveterate gossip. I can't wait to get off this train and tell everyone I know everything I've heard!"

On a Sunday morning, a mother went to wake her son for church.

"I'm not going," he said, and turned over.

"Holy Mother, why not?" said she.

Now he sat up. "I'll tell you why not. One, they don't like me and, two, I don't like them. Why should I go?"

"Begorrah, I'll tell you why. One, you're 59 years old and, two, you're the parish priest."

The Rabbi and the Priest in Belfast were old friends and their congregations often held socials together.

At the annual picnic, the priest teased the rabbi, saying, "What a shame you can't eat ham or bacon. It's so delicious! And Mrs. O'Riley knows exactly how to make a baked ham special with cloves and mustard and a hint of brown sugar." The rabbi smiled but was unmoved.

"So tell me, my friend, when are you finally going to break down and try some delicious Irish ham?"

The rabbi gave him a big grin.

"Why, at your wedding, of course!"

The Kindergarten class at St. Brendon's was having a class in art. One little girl was very intent on her drawing.

Sister Mary Kate came over and said, "What is it you're drawing, Eileen?"

"God," said the little girl.

"God, is it? But nobody knows what God looks like!"

Without stopping what she was doing or blinking an eye, the little girl said,

"They will in a minute."

Father Dooley walking down the street saw young Alfred O'Dowd across the street. He was standing on tiptoes, trying to ring the doorbell on a house.

He even tried jumping up to reach it, but he was much too small.

Smiling, Father Dooley crossed the street and came up behind the lad.

"Here, let me help you, Alfred," he said, and gave the doorbell a mighty push.

Then, squatting down to the boy's height, he said, "And now what, young man?"

"And now, Father," said Alfred.

"Now we run like the devil!"

[273]

A nun who really needed to pee walked into the local pub. As soon as she entered, all the laughing and singing stopped. She was self-conscious, but she really had to go.
"Please, may I use your restroom?"
The barkeep said, "I must warn you, there's a picture of a naked man in there, with his private parts covered by a fig leaf."
"I shall look the other way," she said; and went to use the rest room. When she came back, the laughter and singing stopped again, followed by a round of applause.
The barkeep explained: "Every time the fig leaf on the picture is moved aside, the lights all go out. Now that you're one of us, how about a drink on the house?"

A businessman enters a tavern, sits at the bar and orders a double Martini. When the drink is finished, he peeks into his shirt pocket and asks the bartender to bring him another. When that glass is empty, he does a repeat. Asked about this, he says, "It's a picture of my wife. When she begins to look good, I know it's time to go home."

A SMALL COLLECTION OF BLESSINGS, CURSES, AND THE ODD THOUGHT

May the road rise up to meet you
May the wind be always at your back
May the sun shine down upon your face
And the rain fall soft upon your fields
Until we meet again
May God hold you in the hollow of his hand.

Here's to our wives and girlfriends!
May they never meet!

May those who love us love us
And those that don't love us,
May God turn their hearts;
If he can't turn their hearts, may he
Turn their ankles, so we'll know them
By their limping.

May you live as long as you want...and never
want as long as you live.

Here's to a long life and a merry one,
A quick death and a an easy one.
A pretty girl and an honest one
A cold beer and another one.

These are the things I wish for you:
Someone to love; some work to do;
A bit o' sun; a bit o' cheer.
And a guardian angel, always near.

For the home:
Walls for the wind
And a roof for the rain,
And drink beside the fire.
Laughter to cheer you
And those you love near you
And all that your heart may desire!

A man who is not afraid of the sea will soon
be drowned.

Blood is thicker than water...and easier seen.

If you're lucky enough to be Irish... you're lucky enough.

May your blessings outnumber
The shamrocks that grow
And may trouble avoid you
Wherever you go.

May the Irish hills caress you,
May her lakes and rivers bless you.

May we both be alive at this time next year!

May your purse always hold a coin or two.
May the sun always shine on your windowpane.
May a rainbow be certain to follow each rain.
May the hand of a friend always be near you.
May God fill your heart with gladness to cheer you.

Leprechauns, castles, good luck and
laughter.
Lullabies, dreams and love ever after
A thousand welcomes when anyone comes...
That's the Irish for you!

May the roof above you never fall in and
those gathered beneath it never fall out.

Father O'Leary is a new priest and he asks
Father Finn, the older priest, to sit in while
he hears confessions.
Father Finn agrees. After a couple of day,
he says to Father O'Leary: "Cross your arms
across your chest. Now say 'Hmmm...I
see...that's too bad."
Father O'Leary follows his instructions.
"Very good," says the old priest. "Now isn't
that better than slapping your knee and
saying 'No, shit! What happened next?'"

Adam and Eve had an ideal marriage. He
didn't have to hear about the men she could
have married and she didn't have to hear
about his mother's great cooking.

[278]

A soldier ran up to a nun and asked if he might hide under the skirt of her habit. "I'm a dead man if you don't help," he said; so she agreed.

A moment later, the Military Police ran up and asked, "Sister, have you seen a soldier pass this way?"

"He went that way," lied the nun.

After the MPs had left, the soldier crawled out. "Thank you so much, sister. They're after sending me to Afghanistan."

The nun said, "I understand completely."

The soldier added, "I don't want to be rude, but you have a great pair of legs."

The nun replied: "If you had looked a little higher, you'd have seen a great pair of balls. I don't want to go there, either."

Father Egan answers his phone. "Is this Father Timothy Egan?"

"It is."

"This is the tax people. Do you have a Teddy Houlihan in your church?"

"I do."A

"Did he give 10,000 Euro to the church?"

"He will."

Brian was found dead in his back yard, and the weather was a bit on the warm side. The wake was held down to two days, so his mortal remains wouldn't take a bad turn. His friends bundled him into the box and started down the hill to the churchyard. As if was a long sloping path and the mourners were tipsy, one fellow bumped into the gatepost as they entered the graveyard. Suddenly, a loud knocking came from the coffin. Brian was alive! They opened the box and he sat up and they all said, "Sure and, it's a miracle!" All rejoiced and had a few more drinks to celebrate. But later that day, the poor lad died. Really died. So they put him back into his box and as they huffed and puffed down the hill the next morning, the priest said, "Careful now, boys, mind ya don't bump that gatepost again!"

After the 10 o'clock mass at St. Mary's, a stranger shook the priest's hand. "That was a damn fine mass," he said. "Mind yer language," said the priest. "So fine that I left 500 pounds in the collection plate." "No shit!" said the priest.

[280]

A nicely turned-out young woman on a flight from Ireland to JFK asked the priest sitting next to her, "Father, may I ask a favor?"
"Of course, child, What may I do for you?'
"I bought myself an expensive hair dryer in Dublin for the mother's birthday. It's unopened and well over the Customs limit. I'm afraid they'll confiscate it. Is there any way you could carry it through Customs… under your robe, perhaps?"
"I would like to help you, my dear, but I must warn you … I will not lie."
"Oh, I'm sure with your cassock and honest face, no one will question you. Thank you so much."
When they got to Customs, the woman let the priest go ahead of her. The official asked, "Father, do you have anything to declare?'
Said the priest, "From the top of my head to my waist, I have nothing to declare."
Puzzled, the official asked, "And from your waist to the floor…anything?"
"I have a marvelous instrument designed to be used on a woman, but which is, to date… unused."

Moira Clancy and her little girl were on a trip to New York City. It was the first time little Daphne had ever been out of Ireland and she had a million questions. The mother hailed a cab to take them downtown to the Statue of Liberty ferry and kept fielding her daughter's questions.

When they got to a questionable part of town, the little girl said "Who are all those ladies wearing shorts in the cold, Mammy?"

Moira said, "Oh, they're dancers, darling, and they're waiting for their husbands to come in the car to pick them up."

The cabbie snarled, "Aw, c'mon, lady, tell the kid the truth! They're hookers, plain and simple! Dancers! Husbands! Ha!"

After a silence, the child said, "Do these ladies have any kids, Mammy?"

"Of course," said her mother, sweetly. "Where do you think American cabbies come from?"

Going to church doesn't make you a Christian any more than standing in the garage makes you a car.

[282]

Father McGee walked into his church and saw a man sitting cross-legged in front of the altar.

"My son," he said. "What are you doing there? Who are you?"

Said the stranger, "I'm God." "Pardon?"

"I'm God," repeated the man. "This is my house."

Father McGee ran into the presbytery in a panic and called his bishop. "There's a man in my church," he explained, "Who insists that he's God. What on earth shall I do?"

"Take no chances," said the bishop. "Get back into the church and look busy."

Four nuns were waiting to get into heaven. St. Peter asks if any of them have sinned. "Once I looked at a penis," said one. "Wash your eyes in this holy water and enter heaven," said the saint. The second nun had held a man's penis. She washed that hand in holy water and was admitted. The fourth nun pushed ahead of number three. Why, she was asked, was she so rude?

"Because I want to gargle in that holy water before she sits in it."

Murphy walked up to a Franciscan and Jesuit brother who were talking together, and asked, "How many novenas must I say to get a Mercedes Benz?"
The Franciscan asked, "What's a Mercedes Benz?"
The Jesuit asked, "What's a novena?"

A little boy was becoming bored with a long sermon filled with big words. Then the red sanctuary light caught his eye. Tugging his father's sleeve, he said, "Da, when the light turns green, can we go?"

Jesus was walking along a road in Judea one day when he came upon a group of people surrounding a woman. It was obvious that the crowd was preparing to stone her, so Jesus made his now-famous statement, "Let the person who has no sin cast the first stone." The crowd, shamed, began to turn away one by one. Suddenly, a little woman made her way through the crowd and tossed a pebble toward the woman.
Jesus said, "I really hate it when you do that, Mom."

The Pope is visiting Dublin and is picked up at the airport by a limousine. He begs the driver to let him drive, since he rarely gets to do that. The driver is, of course, hesitant; but how do you say "NO" to the Pope?

So they change places and the Pope starts driving. It turns out he is a speed demon and is caught driving 100 kph in a 45 kph zone.

Kelly, the cop, demands he roll down his window and when he does, the policeman turns white with surprise.

"Pardon, sor, but I must talk to me superior." He goes back to his car and speaks with his chief on the radio.

Cop: Chief, I have a problem. I pulled over this guy for driving much too fast but it's someone very important.

Chief: Important? Like the President?

Cop: No, no. Much more important than that.

Chief: Well, come on, man, just tell me who it is and let's be done with it!

Cop: I'm not sure who he is, but he's got the Pope driving for him!

[285]

A Catholic boy and a Jewish boy were chatting and the Catholic boy said, "My priest knows more than your rabbi."
The Jewish boy said, "Of course he does; you tell him everything."

Late on a Friday night, Father Malone stumbles into a monastery and requests shelter there.
He's just in time for dinner and is treated to the best fish and chips he has ever tasted.
After dinner he goes into the kitchen to thank the chefs.
He is met by two brothers, Brother Michael and Brother Francis.
"I'm very pleased to meet you, Brothers," says Father Malone. "I just wanted to thank you for a wonderful dinner.
"Begorrah, the fish and chips were out of this world! Tell me, which one of you cooked them?"
Brother Michael replies: "I'm the fish friar."
Father Malone turns to the other brother and says, "Then you must be..."
"Yes, I'm afraid I'm the chip monk..."

After the baptism of his baby brother in church, little Ronan sobbed all the way home. His father tried in vain to get him to say what was amiss.

Finally, the little boy said, "Father O'Hara said he wanted us brought up in a Christian home, but I want to stay with you guys!"

A man in Belfast is on the roof of a tall building. A Garda rushes up and shouts, "Don't jump! Think of your Mammy!"
"Got no Mammy. I'm gonna jump."
The Garda runs through every relative he can think of: father, wife, son, daughter, cousins. Nothing works. Then he shouts: "Think of the blessed Virgin!"
"Who is that?"
Garda yells, "Jump, ye Protestant lump! You're blockin' traffic!"

An elderly man bursts into the priest's study.
"I'm having an affair! At my age!"
"How long since your last confession?"
"I'm Jewish," says the man.
"Then why are you telling me this?"
"I'm telling everyone!"

[287]

Years ago, there was an anti-British priest in Dublin who was notorious for spewing hatred from the pulpit every Sunday.

Finally, his Archbishop called him in and forbade him from ever mentioning the British people in public again. He was made to swear by the blessed Virgin. Bitterly he did so.

On the very next Easter Sunday, he was in the pulpit, telling the Easter story to his congregation.

He got to the part where Jesus said, "And one of you shall betray me."

The priest continued: "St. Andrew jumps up and says, 'Is it I Lord?' and Jesus says, 'Nay, Andy darlin', not you. Sit down now and dunna worry. Eat your supper.'

"Then St. John the Divine gets up with tears in his eyes and cries, 'Is it I, Lord?' and Jesus says, 'Nay, Johnny me boyo, it's not you. Sit down now and dunna fret yourself.'

"Then," the priest continued, with venom in his voice, "then that dirty dog Judas Iscariot slooowly rises to his feet and he looks Jesus right in the eye and says, 'Blimey, mate. Ya think it's me?'"

[288]

Late one night, a burglar broke into a house in Galway he thought was empty. He was tiptoeing through the lounge when he heard a voice say loudly, "Jesus is watching you!" He stopped dead. Then silence. The burglar continued creeping. "Jesus is watching you!" boomed the voice again. Now he was scared and then, peering through the dim light, he saw a large cage in the corner. In the cage was a parrot.

"Was that you who said Jesus is watching?"

"Yes," said the parrot.

The burglar breathed a sigh of relief.

"Alright, then. What's yer name?"

"Clarence," the parrot said.

"Clarence! That's a dumb name for a bird! What eejit named you that?"

"The same eejit who named the Doberman Jesus."

Two Jesuit novices both wanted a cigarette while praying. The first asked and was told No. He spotted the other smoking and asked, "Why are you allowed and not me?" "Because you asked to smoke while praying and I asked if I could pray while smoking."

Children lined up in the cafeteria of a Catholic elementary school in Ballyvaughn for lunch. At the head of the table was a large pile of apples with a note, posted by a nun, saying: "Take only ONE. God is watching." At the other end of the table was a large pile of chocolate biscuits.
A child had written a note saying: "Take all you want. God is watching the apples."

A man collapsed from a major heart attack on a Dublin street and was taken to St. Bridget's Hospital where he had open-heart surgery. When he waked, there was a nun sitting by his bed. She had taken his vital signs and felt he could answer some questions about paying for his treatment.
"I haven't got health insurance," he rasped.
"Then perhaps some money in the bank?"
He replied: "No money in the bank."
"Do you have family who might help you?"
"I have only a spinster sister who is a nun."
The nun became agitated and announced loudly, "Nuns are not spinsters! Nuns are married to God!"
"Then send the bill to my brother-in-law!"

short
and
snappy

THE BEST OF IRISH HUMOR

You'd better not iron your four-leaf clovers. You wouldn't want to press your luck.

Did you know? People wear shamrocks on St. Patrick's Day because regular rocks are too heavy.

You can tell an Irishman is having a good time when he's Dublin over with laughter.

You know, the reason you can't borrow money from a leprechaun is because they're always a little short.

What do you get when you cross a pillowcase with a stone?
A shamrock.

An Irishman who can control his wife is called a bachelor.

A river is rich because it has two banks.

When is an Irish potato not an Irish potato?
When it's a French fry!

The first Irish National Steeplechase was
finally abandoned. Not one horse could get
a decent footing on the cathedral roof.

Concerning bagpipes:
The Irish invented them and gave them to
the Scots as a joke. The Scots haven't seen
the joke yet.

An Irish professor was in Spain. His host
asked if the Irish had a word in their
language similar to manana. Sure, said the
professor, we have five words similar to
manana; but none of them with quite the
same sense of urgency.

"Mary, how do you like your new false
teeth?" asks Colleen.
"I'm leaving them out 'til I get used to
them."

"I hear O'Brien died," says Pat. "Was he ill long?"
"No," says Mick. "He died in the best of health."

The doctor was puzzled. "I'm so sorry, Mr. O'Toole, but I can't diagnose your problem. I think it must be drink."
"Don't worry about it, doctor. I'll come back when you're sober," said O'Toole.

Where were you going when I saw you coming back?
I ran after you, but when I caught up to you, you were gone.

You three are a right pair if ever I saw one!

"How far is it to the next village?" asked the American tourist.
"About seven miles," guessed the farmer.
"But it's only five if you run."

I'm so unlucky that I bought a non-stick pan and then I couldn't get the label off.

I'd like some nails," said Timothy. "How long would you like them?" asked the tinker. "Forever, if that's all right with you."

I was going to give her a nasty look, but she already had one.

What's the difference between an Irish wedding and an Irish wake?
One less drunk.

In an Irish courtroom, 12 men sat on the jury. After the trial, the Judge asked for their verdict. "We find that man who stole the horse 'Not Guilty'," said the foreman.

A moon is going broke when it's down to its last quarter.

An Irish lass in the dress store: "Could I be trying on that dress in the window?"
Shopkeeper: "I'd prefer that you use the dressing room."

Mrs. Leary shouted from the kitchen, "Is that you I hear spittin' in the vase on the mantelpiece?"
"No," said himself. "But I'm gettin' closer all the time."

Due to a water shortage in Ireland, Dublin swimming baths plan to close lanes 5 and 6.

Dooley bought himself a jigsaw puzzle with twenty pieces. It took him a month to put it together. He was very proud, but his mate, Murphy, said, "What's so good about that?"
"Well, on the box, it said '4 to 6 years.'"

If I ever go missing, put my picture on a beer can. I want fun people to find me.

At the Cheltenham racing festival, Noonan leaned over and whispered to his friend Clancy, "Now would you be wanting the winner of the next race?"
"No, thanks," said Clancy. "I've only got a small yard."

"Shay, do you understand German?"
"To be sure I do, if it's spoken in Irish."

"Oh, that was a lovely dress," said Maureen, "and it would have fitted me if I could have got into it, so it would!"

A man, half Irish, half Scottish, wants a pint; but can't bring himself to pay for it.

Doonan and Noonan have just opened a new restaurant on the moon. It serves great cheese, but the atmosphere is terrible.

Why did the Irishman buy a black and white dog? He thought the license would be cheaper.

"O'Halloran," said the pharmacist, "did that mudpack I gave you improve your wife's appearance?"

"It did surely," said O'Halloran, "but it keeps fallin' off."

Finnegan was arrested and sent for trial for armed bank robbery.

After due deliberation, the jury foreman stood up and announced, "Not guilty."

"That's grand!" shouted Finnegan. "Does that mean I get to keep the money?"

Donncha is shocked at finding out all his cows are suffering from "Bluetongue."

"Bejabbers, I didn't know they had mobile phones."

Harrigan is walking through a graveyard when he comes across a headstone with the inscription: "Here lies a politician and an honest man."

"Faith now," mutters Harrigan. "I wonder how they got the two of them in one grave?"

Farmer One: My cow fell down a hole and I had to shoot it.
Farmer Two: In the hole?
Farmer One: No, in the head.

Pauline Meeham was keeping a close eye on her new neighbors. "They seem perfectly devoted to each other," she opined to husband Brian. "He kisses her every time he goes out and even blows kisses to her from the car window. Why don't you do that?"
"But I hardly know the woman!" said Brian.

"What's wrong with Murphy?"
"Yesterday he swallowed a spoon and he hasn't stirred since."

"Why do you Irish always answer a question with a question?" asked President F.D. Roosevelt.
"Do we now?" came NY Mayor Al Smith's reply.

Grow your own dope. Plant a man.

Nolan was in the hospital, swathed in bandages from head to foot. "By God, what happened to ye?" asked Gallagher.
"I staggered out of the Invincible pub, and a lorry hit me a glancing blow and knocked me through the plate glass window."
"Begorrah," exclaimed Gallagher, "It's a good job you were wearing all those bandages or you'd have been cut to ribbons!"

If two's company and three's a crowd, what's four and five?
Nine.

O'Malley lost $100 on the Melbourne Cup, a famous Australian horse race.
He also lost another hundred on the television replay.

Did you hear about the Irishman who was tap dancing?
He broke his ankle when he fell into the sink.

"That's it!" said McCarthy, leaving the dentist's office. "I've just had all me teeth out. Never again!"

Irish sailor, shipwrecked, saw a lifeboat washed ashore. He built a raft from it.

Connally always slept with his gun under his pillow. Hearing a noise at the foot of his bed, he got his gun and shot off his big toe. "Thank the Lord I wasn't sleeping at the other end of the bed," he said to his friends in the pub.
 "I would have blown my head off."

Quinn sells Flynn a donkey.
Some weeks later, they meet in a pub and Flynn says, "Hey, Quinn, that donkey you sold me went and died."
Quinn sips his Guinness slowly and says, "Bejabbers, Flynn, it never done that on me."

Kelly was getting irate and shouted upstairs to his wife, "Hurry up or we'll be late!"
"Oh, be quiet," shouted his wife, "Haven't I been telling you for the last hour that I'll be ready in a minute?"

An Irish spaceman is a lunartic.

Why don't Irish women use vibrators?
They chip their teeth.

Did you hear about the Irish water polo team?
All their horses drowned.

How do two Irishmen change a light bulb?
One holds the bulb and the other starts drinking until the room spins.

An Irishman walked into Macy's and asked for the cheapest suit they had.
The sales clerk replied: "You're wearing it."

What are the best ten years of an Irishman's life?
Third grade.

A sign says "Tree fellers wanted."
Pat says to Mike, "Bejesus, it's a shame there's only two of us."

"I'll have fish and chips twice," announced Flaherty.
"Very well," said the shopkeeper. "The fish won't be long."
"Well, they'd best be fat," said Flaherty.

Finegan says there are twice as many eyebrows in the world as people.

"Good morning, Mrs. Irwin, and how is everything?"
"Sure, and I'm having a great time of it between my husband and the fire.
"If I keep my eye on the one, the other is sure to go out."

[304]

"There's a terrible smell in this café," said O'Hara.
"Maybe it's the drains."
"It can't be the drains," retorted O'Hara. "We haven't got any."

"I had an accident opening a can of alphabet spaghetti this morning," says Moran.
"Were you hurt?" asks Murphy.
"No, but it could've spelled disaster."

Why did God invent Jameson whiskey?
So the Irish would never rule the world.

How did the Irish jig get started?
Too much to drink and not enough toilets.

"I married an Irishman on St. Patrick's Day." "Oh, really?"
"No, O'Riley."

Frogs love St. Patrick's Day because they're always wearing green.

[305]

What does a leprechaun call a happy man wearing green?
Jolly Green Giant.

The late Bishop Sheen figured that the Irish fight each other so much is because they're sure of having a worthy opponent.

Getting rid of an Irishman without hurting his pride can be touchy. Try saying "I love you, I want to marry you and have your children."
Sometimes they leave skid marks.

You know it's an Irishman if he never kisses his wife but will kill anyone else who does.

What is Barney's favorite thing in Eire? A BLARNEY stone, of course.

Are people jealous of the Irish?
To be sure, they're green with envy.

[306]

What does it mean when you find a horseshoe?
Some poor horse is going barefoot.

Why did St. Patrick drive all the snakes out of Ireland?
He couldn't afford airfare.

IN IRELAND:
.A sub-standard dwelling is called a kip.

.To ask someone to be quiet, say "Whisht!"

.For emphasis, the word "fierce" is often used, or "wicked." "It's wicked warm today."

When Irish eyes are smiling, they're usually up to something.

I had an Irish dog that chased parked cars.

Nothing is foolproof to a sufficiently talented fool.

IRISH COLLEGE HUMOR

Q. Why don't they have Christmas at Trinity?
A. They can't find a virgin and three wise men.

Q. What do you get when you drive quickly through the Carlow campus?
A. An undergraduate degree.

Q. What's the first thing a Trinity girl does when she wakes up in the morning?
A. Walks home.

Q. Did you hear that the library at Burren College burned down?
A. Naturally, the students were very upset. Some of the books weren't colored in yet.

Q. How do you get an IT grad off your front porch? A. Pay him for the pizza.

Q. What do tornadoes and graduates from Griffith have in common?
A. They both end up in trailer parks.

[308]

Q. What does an IT student call a Trinity student after graduation?
A. Boss.

Q. How to separate the men from boys at All Hallows.
A. With a restraining order.

How we know that light travels faster than sound: Because some people appear bright until you hear them speak.

Change is inevitable, except from a vending machine.

Those who live by the sword get shot by those who don't.

The shin bone is for finding furniture in the dark.

If you lined up all the cars in the world end to end, someone would be stupid enough to try to pass them.

If the shoe fits, get another one just like it.

The things that come to those who wait will be the things left by those who got there first.

Q: Can I speak English wherever I go in Ireland?
A: Just so long as you learn it first.

Irish Paddy and Scot Jock were both in the Army and were being made to double-time march around the public square.
The breathless Jock said: "Aye, Paddy, I no like 'doublin'."
"Well," answered Paddy, "I'm not too keen on Edinborough, either."

You can't kiss an Irish girl unexpectedly. You can only kiss her sooner than she thought you would.

Did you hear how Ireland solved their unemployment problem?
They now stay in school until age 65.

The Dubliner working in a banana importer was fired for throwing out all the bent ones.

TEACHER: Donal, do you pray before eating?
DONAL: I don't have to. My Mammy's a good cook.

"Tell me, Tom," asked the parish priest. "How did you manage to get so very drunk last night?
"I got into very bad company, Father, after winning a bottle of whisky at a raffle."
"But I know the fellows you were with and none of them drink."
"That's the problem, Father."

[311]

Always the opportunist, Higgins walked all the way to the heart of Australia because he heard it was virgin territory.

An Irishman was wandering around JFK, tears streaming down his face. A guard asked what happened.
"I lost me luggage."
"That's terrible, sir. How did it happen?"
"Cork fell out."

"The government's had our backs against the wall," says Hooligan. "It's time we turned around and fought!"

Bridey O'Grady had an exorcism, but she couldn't pay for it. So she was repossessed.

Where can you find the blood relations of an Englishman?
In the family tree.
Where can you find the blood relations of an Irishman?
In the Dublin Phone Registry.

A good time to keep your mouth shut is when you're in deep water.

If you don't have a sense of humor, you probably don't have any sense at all.

The visiting priest waxed eloquent during the offertory prayer, looking toward heaven as he declaimed: "Without you we are but dust..."
At that very moment, a child's voice asked: "Mammy, what's butt dust?"

The boss looked over the shoulder of his new secretary from Kerry.
"Your typing has improved, I see," he remarked. "That's very good; only five mistakes. Now, please try the second word."

Brenda Murphy found her husband standing in front of their full-length mirror, with his eyes tightly shut.
"Mike, what're you doing?"
"Trying to see what I look like asleep."

Gone are the days when Irish girls cooked like their mothers. Now they drink like their fathers.

McMurphy rang up his local cinema to get viewing times. When the manager answered, McMurphy said, "Is that the local cinema?"
The manager said, "Depends where you're calling from."

You can tell a lot about an Irishwoman's mood just by looking at her hands.
For instance, if they are holding a gun, she's probably not happy.

You know that tingly little feeling you get when you like someone you've just met?
That's common sense leaving your body.

Sometimes you have to burn a few bridges to keep the crazies from following you.

[314]

Some days, the only good thing about my job is that the chair spins.

Says O'Neill: I'm not sayin' let's go kill all the stupid people. I'm sayin' let's remove all the warning labels and let the problem sort itself out.

If you had three apples and four oranges in one hand and four apples and three oranges in the other hand, what would you have? Very large hands.

Teacher: Why are you late, Brendan?
Brendon: Class started before I got here.

How can you drop a raw egg on a concrete floor without cracking it?
Any way you like. Concrete is hard to crack.

The 50-50-50 rule: Any time you have a 50-50 chance of getting something right, there's a 50% probability you'll get it wrong.

Whiskey won't cure a cold but it's a great way to fail.

WHAT IT MEANS TO BE IRISH

.You will never play pro basketball.

.You can outswear anyone.

.At least one of your relatives is a cop, fireman, bar owner, funeral home owner or holds political office.

.You think you sing very well.

.You have no idea how to make a long story short.

.Many of your childhood meals were boiled.

.You're strangely poetic after a few beers.

.You are therefore poetic a lot.

.You will be punched for no good reason... a lot.

.Many of these punches are the legacies of past generations.

.A lot of your female relatives will be named Mary, Catherine, or Eileen... and at least one relative is called Mary Catherine Eileen.

.Someone in your family is incredibly cheap. It is more than likely you.

.You can't wait for the other guy to stop talking for you to start.

.There wasn't a huge difference between your last wake and your last keg party.

.You are, or know someone, named Murph.

.If you don't know Murph, you know Mac.
And if you don't know Mac, you know Sully.
Then you probably know Sully MacMurphy.
.You have Irish Alzheimer's. You forget
everything but the grudges.
.You are genetically incapable of keeping a
secret.
.You may not know the words, but that
doesn't stop you from singing.
.Your favorite "Irish Stew" is a euphemism
for "boiled leftovers."
.All of your losses are alcohol-related...loss of
virginity, loss of driver's license, loss of
money, job, significant other, and loss of
teeth from fighting. But it never stops you
from drinking.

Maureen: Doctor, doctor, I forgot to take
my contradictory pills!
Doctor: You seem to be ignorant.
Maureen: Yes. Three months, I think.

Maura to her mother: "Mammy, I'm
pregnant."
Her mother says,
"Are you sure it's yours?"

Maureen has had six kids.
 "Why don't you use the pill?" asks her
friend Eileen.
 "I do," she says,
"But it keeps falling out."

How come every time you ring a wrong
number, it's never engaged?

Lonigan found his wife in bed with the
lodger. He put a gun to his own head and
said, "What are you laughing about? You're
next!"

Clooney thought a cubicle was a square
testicle.

There's an Irish tale called The Stupid
Prince. He stayed a frog his entire life.

The Irish firing squad formed a circle. When
that didn't work, they lined up one behind
the other.

Sullivan fell 200 feet down a well.
"Have you broken anything?" his boss yelled down.
"No sir, there's nothing down here to break."

The Irishman who stole a calendar got twelve months.

Irish dog sitting by the fire, chewing on a bone. When he stands up, his leg falls off.

A guy in a pub puts a note on his glass of Guinness saying "I spit in this drink." Then he goes to the rest room. When he comes back, there's another note: "So did I."

Two IRA veterans were having a pint in their local pub and listening to the news, when an account of a new outbreak of hostilities up North was announced. "'Tis a terrible war," said one.
"Aye, but 'tis better than no war at all!"

[319]

MURPHY'S LAWS OF DO-IT-YOURSELF

Any project will require at least two more trips to the hardware store.

If you need multiples of any item, the probability that one will be the wrong color or damaged is directly proportional to the need or desire of that object.

You always need more paint. No exceptions.

You're always short one nail or screw in an odd size. No other nail or screw in your household will fit.

The likelihood that you will complete a weekend project before the end of the weekend decreases with every hour you wait to start.

Therefore: any plumbing project begun after 4:00 PM on Sunday will require an emergency call to the plumber to get the water running again.

[320]

To estimate the time needed to complete a project, estimate time needed, multiply by two and use the next highest unit.
Hence: an hour's task will take at least two days to complete.

IN IRELAND
.Wayward children are never called naughty. They are bold.

.To be tired or broken down is to be banjaxed or knackered.

.To procrastinate or delay something is to put it on the long finger.

.If someone is annoying you, they are blaggarding.

.To ask someone to be quiet, you might say "Whisht!"

.A scratcher is a bed, the jacks is a toilet.

.Finishing something fairly lively is fast.

The worst pupil in any class will be a school governor's (principal's) son.

Uniforms come in only two sizes: too large and too small.

Vital documents that were posted with no errors will develop errors in the mail.

A woman in Ballyvaughn gave birth to triplets.
Her husband is still looking for the other two guys.

Why do men come home drunk and leave their clothes on the floor? They're in them.

God, why did you make woman desirable?
So you would love her.
But God, why did you make her so dumb?
So she would love you.

Tourist question: Which way is North in Ireland? Answer: Face South, and then turn 180 degrees. Contact us when you get there and we'll have the rest of the directions.

The other queue always moves faster.

The traffic warden in Galway booked a steamroller for having bald tires.

What do you call an Irishman who has 1500 girlfriends.
A shepherd.

What do you call a Dubliner on a bicycle?
A dope pedaller.

The Irish goldfish: it drowned.

Q: I have developed a Fountain of Youth. Can you tell me where in Ireland I can sell it successfully?
A: Anywhere significant number of Kerrymen gather.

[323]

Sign in an Irish pub:
This establishment closes at 11 o'clock sharp. We are open from 10 AM until 11 PM, and if you haven't had enough to drink at that hour the management feels you haven't really been trying.

An Irish parachute: opens on impact.

How do you get an Irishman on the roof?
Tell him that drinks are on the house.

The Irish Robin Hood fired an arrow in the air... And missed.

What do you call an Irish brain surgeon?
A chiropodist.

How many wonderful Irishmen does it take to do the dishes?
Both of them.

[324]

Did you hear about the Irishman who spent seven years at university and ended up with an IQ equal to none?

Show me a man with both feet planted firmly on the ground, and I will show you a man who can't get his pants off.

Pat says to Mike, "Mike, do you know you only actually use one-third of your brain?" Mike says, "Well, what do you do with the other half?"

Why did the Irish get potatoes and the Arabs got oil?
Because the Irish got first pick.

What about the Irish woodworm?
Found dead in a brick.

How do you get an Irishman to laugh on Sunday? Tell him a joke on Friday night!

How do you confuse an Irishman?
Put him in a barrel and tell him to piss in a corner.

A man who is not afraid of the sea will soon be drowned.

Asked to spell "paint," the Irishman asked, "Excuse me, sir, but what colour?"

Irish scientists have discovered that birthdays are good for you. The more you have, the longer you live.

Try to say "Irish wristwatch." Then try saying it fast, several times in a row.

An Irish two-seater light aircraft crashed into a cemetery.
Irish search and rescue workers recovered more than 1200 bodies.

In order to get a bank loan, you must first prove that you don't need the money.

Your lost needle will be found by your husband when he is walking around the house barefoot.

Q What's the difference between men and pigs? A Pigs don't get drunk and act like men.

Blood is thicker than water...and more easily seen.

Murphy changed his car horn to the sound of gunshots. He says people move out of his way much faster now.

Five frogs sitting on a log. Four decide to jump off. How many are left?
Answer: five. Why?
Because there's a difference between deciding and doing.

We attract what we love and what we fear.

A family of Irish birth will argue and fight
But let a shout
Come from without
And see them all unite.

All women become like their mothers.
That's their tragedy.
No man does. That's his.

The best way to get rid of your enemies is
God's way—by loving them.

If you're the only one knows that you're
afraid, you're brave.

Better fifty enemies outside the house than
one within it.

If wars were fought with words, Ireland
would be ruling the world.

Three Irishmen walked out of a bar.
IT CAN HAPPEN.

I'm sick of all the Irish stereotypes. As soon as I finish this drink, I'm punching someone.

Now don't you be talkin' about yourself while you're here.
We'll surely be doin' that after you leave.

What do you call an Irishan who keeps bouncing off the wall? Rick O'Shea.

To me, says Fergus, "drink responsibly" means don't spill it.

In twenty years, the Irish will probably declare war on the English. They will have started to understand all the jokes.

The Irish now have a new program for people who want to stop smoking. It's called Nicotine Anonymous. If you get the urge to smoke, they send someone over and you get drunk together.

What's written on the top of an Irish ladder?
STOP.

A day without sunshine is like a day in
Ireland.

What's written on the bottom of a Guiness
bottle?
Open Other End.

What's written on the top of a Guiness
bottle?
See Other End for Instructions.

Vatican Press Release:
Be all women informed that lying in bed,
naked, entangled with somebody and
screaming "Oh my God, Oh my God!" will
NOT be considered praying.

The old-fashioned Irishwoman moved into
her first high-rise home.
It took her three weeks to scrub the front
steps.

Two Irishmen are comparing jobs. One says "I have a twelve hour day from 6:00 in the morning to 6:00 at night."
The other says, "I have a fourteen hour day from 7:00 in the morning until 7:00 at night."

Father Kelly says: Contrary to popular belief, "Dammit" is not God's last name.

Marie O'Donnell hates it when old people poke her at weddings and say, "You're next." She's started to do the same to them at funerals.

The Irish Traffic Experiment before joining the Common Market:
We will drive on the right starting next Sunday.
If the experiment is a success, we will extend it to include cars as well as buses and lorries.
It didn't work.

Only Irish Coffee provides in a single glass all four essential food groups: alcohol, caffeine, sugar, and fat.

Why do they give a 30 minute lunch break to workers in Ireland?
Because if it were any longer, workers would have to be retrained for the afternoon's work.

And then there was the Irish letter bomber who put his name and address on the back of the parcel marked IN CASE OF NON-DELIVERY.

Murphy says he slept like a log last night... he woke up in the fireplace.

O'Hara went to the doctor and asked, "Have you got anything for wind?" And the doctor gave him a kite.

Went to the corner shop ... bought four corners.

[332]

Due to current economic conditions, the light at the end of the tunnel has been turned off. Murphy's graveside service had barely ended when there was a massive clap of thunder followed by a huge bolt of lightning. "Begorrah," said his widow. "He's there!"

Am I ambivalent? Well, yes and no.

A true Irishman has so much respect for the truth that he uses it only in emergencies.

On a tombstone: Here lies an atheist. All dressed up and no place to go

An Englishman, an Irishman, and a Scotsman walked into a bar. Ouch! Ouch! Ouch!

An Englishman, an Irishman, and a Scotsman walked into a bar. The bartender said, "Is this some kind of a joke?"

A conclusion is the place you got tired of thinking.

O'Leary, my neighbor, knocked on my door at 2 AM. Can you believe it? Lucky I was still up playing my bagpipes.

What is six inches long, two inches wide and makes men act like fools?
Money.

Maloney called the hospital maternity floor. "Quick, send an ambulance!" he said. 'My wife is in labor!"
"Is this her first baby?"
"No, this is her husband, Dan, speakin'."

If it took 8 Irishmen 10 hours to build a wall, how long would it take four of them?
No time at all. The wall's already built.

A dog is truly an Irishman's best friend. You don't believe it? Try this. Put your dog and then your wife into the trunk of the car for an hour. When you open the trunk, which one is really glad to see you?

Finn says, "Spread out in a bunch!"

A new bride was a bit embarrassed to be known as a honeymooner. So, at the hotel, she asked her husband how she should act as if she were long married.
"Easy," says he. "You carry the suitcases."

Mary Margaret thought her bank was out of money when they returned her check with the words INSUFFICIENT FUNDS.

Murph said to his wife, Brenda,
"Here's an article in the paper says that women use 30,000 words a day and men use only 15,000."
Brenda: "That's because we have to repeat everything we say."
Murph: "What?"

Why are married women heavier than single women?
Single women come home, see what's in the refrigerator and go to bed.
Married women come home, see what's in the bed and go to the refrigerator.

[335]

A man is sitting in a bar when a beautiful woman walks up and whispers in his ear: "I'll do anything you want for 25 Euros." He puts down his drink and starts going through his pockets, digging up small bills and various coins until he finally has enough. He thrusts the wadded-up money into the woman's hand and says, "Here...paint my house."

Winging his way to the U. S. from Ireland, Murphy asked the attendant, "How high is this plane, Miss?"
"About 32,000 meters," she said.
Murphy's jaw dropped. "Who'd have believed it? And how wide?"

The Irish family that has no skeleton in the cupboard has buried it instead.

No son is as good as his father in his sister's eyes. No father is as good as his son in his mother's eyes.

What I want to be when I'm old: younger.

The man said, "Excuse me, sir, but would you like to become a Jehovah's Witness?"
"Oh, I don't think so," was the reply.
"I didn't even see the accident."

Life isn't about how to survive the storm, but how to dance in the rain.

A boasting American said to O'Hara: "In America, we can erect a block of skyscrapers in about two weeks."
Retorted O'Hara: "That's nothing. We can start a row of houses in the morning and on the way home from work, the bailiff will be there, ousting tenants for being behind in their rent."

Recipe for Irish Stew:
Get some meat and cut into pieces.
Do the same with potatoes.
Get a lot of Guinness Stout.
Drink the stout.
Forget about the rest of it.

Children begin by loving their parents. After a time, they judge them. Rarely, if ever, do they forgive them.   -Oscar Wilde

How many Irishmen does it take to change a lightbulb? Six. One to change it and five to sing about how grand the old one was.

A little Galway girl was in class learning the alphabet, when her teacher asked her, "So, what comes after T?"
"The 6:00 o'clock news," she said.

Then there was the Irish burglar. He broke into the bookies' shop and lost 20 Euros.

It was Mike's first day in a Cork building site and already things weren't going too well. The foreman confused him. He showed him a selection of spades and told him to take his pick.

[338]

Nora O'Banion says she reads recipe the same way she reads science fiction. When she gets to the end, she thinks, "Well, that's not going to happen."

Those who say there's no such thing as a stupid question...they've never worked in Customer Service.

Q: Do you celebrate Christmas in Ireland?
A: Only at Christmas.

How can you lift an elephant with one hand? You will never find an elephant with hands.

Road sign in Tipperary: NOTICE. When this sign is underwater, the road is impassable.

Elderly Matt Flanigan went to the doctor.
"I can't pee," he said.
"How old are you now, Matt?" said the doctor.
"Ninety-two."
"You've pee'ed enough."

Jesus is coming! Look busy.

LEPRECHAUN Q AND A

Q. Why can't you borrow from a leprechaun?
A. Because they're always a little short.

Q. A leprechaun worked at a diner?
A. Yes, he was the short-order cook.

Q. How did a leprechaun beat Paddy to the pot of gold?
A. He took a shortcut.

Q. What do you get when two leprechauns have a conversation?
A. A lot of small talk.

Q. What kind of BBQ do leprechauns like?
A. Short ribs.

Q. Is a leprechaun secretary good?
A. Of course. They're good at shorthand.

Q. Do they get angry when you make fun of their height?
A. Yes, but only a little.

What do you call a clumsy Irish dance?
A jig mistake.

How can you tell an Irishman's having a
good time?
He's Dublin over with laughter.

What does Ireland have more of than any
other country?
Irishmen.

What do you think of my Irish stew?
It could use a bit more Gaelic.

What's big and purple and lies right next to
Ireland?
Grape Britain.

Photons have mass? I didn't even know
they were Catholic.

If you believe you can tell me what to think,
I believe I can tell you where to go.

Those who get too big for their britches will
be exposed in the end.

In Ireland, a secret is something you tell to
only one person at a time.

I had amnesia once. Maybe twice

 "So," said Maureen, "how's your husband?"
"Compared to what?" replied Colleen.

Sean walked into his local barber shop and
asked how much for a haircut.
"Five pounds," said the barber. Sean
thought and then asked, "How much for a
shave?" "Oh, that's only a pound."
"Okay, then," said Sean. "Shave me head."

Four surgeons argued about who was the
easiest kind of patient to operate on. They
decided it was a politician: no guts, no
heart, no spine; and head and arse
interchangeable.

Did you hear the one about the Irishman who tried to repair a gas leak in a hospital? Doctors informed his wife that he was on a life support machine, the bed, the curtains, the window, and all over the walls.

A man on holiday was making his way to the bathroom in Murphy's B&B.
"Excuse me, sir," said Nora Murphy. "Do you have a good memory for faces?"
"The guest stopped at the bathroom door and said, "Yes, I do, actually."
"That's great," said Nora. "Because there's no mirror in the bathroom."

Mullen noticed that Doyle was looking very sad as they met in the street.
"What's the matter, boyo?"
"I've lost me dog," moaned Doyle, "and I can't find him"
"Why don't you put an advert in the paper?"
Mullen stared, bewildered.
"Don't be daft. You know he can't read."

If the world were truly a logical place, then men would be riding sidesaddle.

Dan Houlihan came home looking very upset. "I've been sacked from me job on the one-man bus," he said. "Why?" his wife asked. "Because the bus crashed and they said it was my fault." "How did that happen?" "I don't know," said Houlihan. "I was upstairs collecting fares at the time."

We're not saying he was the smelliest man in Ireland. But when he put odour-eaters in his shoes, in 5 minutes he had disappeared.

Murph went up to the woman behind the counter and said loudly, "I'd like a pint of the black stuff and a packet of cheese and onion crisps, please."
"Sir, this is a library."
"Oh. Sorry." In a whisper he repeated, "I'd like a pint of the black stuff and a packet of cheese and onion crisps, please."

"I just got a loft extension in me apartment," boasted Seamus.
"Oh, dear," said Mary, "That must have been very expensive." "It was," said Seamus. "And it really upset the fella upstairs."

A young man runs into the local pub and shouts, "Call me a doctor! Call me a doctor!"

"What's wrong?" asks the bartender. "Are you ill?"

"No. I've just graduated from medical school!"

Did you hear about the pregnant Irish woman who wanted to have her baby in a big supermarket?
She heard they had free delivery service.

Did you hear about the dyslexic Irish twins?
Every full moon one would turn into a warehouse and the other became an atheist who didn't believe in dog.

Mike Murphy says, "My doctor told me to start killing people. Well, not in those exact words. He said I had to reduce the stress in my life.
"Same thing, really!"

ALL ABOUT SEX

No matter how many times you've had it, if you're offered sex, take it, because it'll never be quite the same again.

The qualities that most attract a woman to a man are usually the same ones she can't stand years later.

If you get them by the balls, their hearts and minds will follow.

Sex is like snow. You never know how many inches you are going to get or how long it is going to last.

Sex appeal is 50% what you've got and 50% what other people think you've got.

Sex takes the least amount of time and causes the most amount of trouble.

"My Dad could beat up your Dad!"
"No big deal! So could my Mum!"

"Excuse me," said O'Dowd. "Do you serve women in this pub?"
"'Fraid not, sor, you'll have to bring your own."

An American tourist walks into a country pub in Tipperary. "Hey, man, what a quaint old Irish pub you got here," he says. "It's got atmosphere and patina and look, it's even got sawdust on the floor!" The barman looks at him. "That's not sawdust, that's last night's furniture."

A farmer in Mayo was trying to raise chickens, but having no luck at all.
"What d'ye think I'm doing wrong?" he asked his wife.
"Maybe you're plantin' them too deep?"

Ann Boyle went to a psychiatrist. He gave her a tranquilizer. After a week, he asked,"How are you?" and Annie said, "Who cares?"

It was Molly Malone's first day working at the restaurant, and the manager called her over.

"Molly, tell me, why has it taken you four hours to fill four salt cellars?"

"Oh, I'm so sorry; but it's hard to get the salt into that little hole at the top."

He who laughs last thinks slowest.

O'Rourke went up before the judge and as he stood in the dock, the judge gave him a long, hard look.

"Tell me, is this the first time you've been up before me?"

"I don't know, your honour," said O'Rourke.

"What time do you usually get up?"

Connelly was very unhappy, even though he'd just sold his house at a very nice profit. His landlord is suing him!

Every Irishman knows:
The first 40 years of childhood are the worst.

"Is that Belfast double-three double-three?" asked the voice when Higgins answered the phone.
"No," said Higgins. "This is Belfast 3333."
"Oh, I'm so sorry to have bothered you."
"Not to worry," said Higgins, "The phone was ringing anyway."

Teacher: Shaun, what do you call a person who talks even when nobody is interested?
Shaun: A teacher.

"Hello," said the man when O'Grady answered his door.
 "I'm collecting for the public baths."
"Just a minute," said O'Grady.
He left the room and came back with a bucket of water.

The head of the Irish Football Association called a press conference.
He said, "I've called you all here today to announce that we have picked the team to represent Ireland at the next World Cup. It's Brazil."

The Galway boy who was rushed to the hospital after eating all the Christmas tree decorations was treated for Tinselitis.

Everyone knows that the English invented the toilet seat in 1643, and very proud of it they were.
Then, in 1645, the Irish added the hole.

A Dublin steamroller driver rushed into the pub, shouting "Can anyone here tell me how tall a penguin is?"
"To be sure," says one patron. "Around two foot six."
"Oh, begorrah!" the driver moaned. "I've run over a nun!"

It's a well-known fact that an Englishman laughs at a joke three times:
once, when everyone he's with gets it; the second time, when, a week later, he thinks he gets it; and finally, a month later when an Irishman explains it to him.

"Have ye seen my new vest, Bridey?"
"Dougal, ya great eejit, you're wearin' it!"
"Good thing ye noticed, or I'd have gone out
without it."

Ireland has solved her unemployment
problem. You stay in school until you're
sixty.

Irish scientists have discovered that we only
use one-quarter of our brain power.
They're still trying to figure out what we do
with the other one quarter.

News flash! An Irishman was killed while
drinking milk
The cow fell on him.

A while ago, there was talk of an Irish Mafia
being set up in Belfast. It didn't last long
because the Godfather, Don Killgallan, kept
making offers he couldn't remember or
understand.

The long-awaited Tug of War between Dublin and Cork was cancelled because they couldn't find a long enough rope.

His family adored him. On every St. Patrick's Day, they would give him a four-leaf poison ivy.

A small boy asked the girl next door, "Are you the opposite sex, or am I?"

Children do not understand adult logic. Why do they have to go to sleep when Mammy gets tired?

Colleen said to Marie: "Whenever I'm down in the dumps, I buy myself a new dress."
Said Marie: "I always wondered where you got them."

One day my wife said, "I'd like to go someplace where I've never been."
I said, "Try the kitchen!"

Did you hear about the Irish Tooth Fairy? She was sacked. She left the tooth under the pillow and then took all the other teeth as well.

Dunaway and Clancy were fishing under the bridge when they heard a rumble overhead. Looking up, they saw a funeral procession making its slow way across the bridge. Dunaway took off his hat and held it over his heart. "That's right respectful of you, Dunaway," said Clancy. "It's the least I could do," Dunaway replied. "We would have been married 28 years this week."

Nolan was so desperate to see the big soccer match that he pushed into the line ahead of people who had been waiting quite a while. A steward stopped him and told him he had to go to the very back of the queue. Nolan did as he was told but very soon he was back again, pushing and shoving. "Oi, there!" shouted the steward. "I thought I told you to go to the back of the queue!" "I did, I did," said Nolan. "But there was already somebody there."

[353]

She sent her picture to a Lonely Hearts Club.
They sent it back. "We're not that lonely."

She's so ugly she has to go to church to
confess it.

FRONT OF A PUB:
Soup of the Day:
WHISKEY!

When your eyesight begins to blur, don't
bother about glasses. Just make your drinks
a bit weaker.

Dear paranoid people who check behind
their shower curtains for murderers.
If you do find one, what's your plan?

I've got to stop saying, "How stupid can you
be? Too many people are taking it as a
challenge.

[354]

At most fancy hotels, they have a big card in the room that asks HAVE YOU LEFT ANYTHING?
What they should be asking is if you've got anything left.

My sister is a waitress at the psychiatric hospital. She serves soups to nuts.

A ragged man approached Hogan and asked for a handout. Hogan said, "You'll only waste the money on drink or drugs."
The man said, "No, I need it for food. I don't drink, I don't do drugs, and I don't gamble."
"Really? Well, come with me to my house and I'll give you five pounds."
When they got to Hogan's house, Hogan knocked on the door and his wife Kathleen answered.
She stared at the two of them and said, "What's this about, then?"
Hogan said,
"I just wanted you to see what happens to a man who doesn't smoke or drink or do drugs or gamble."

Sister Mary Josephine, teaching Sunday
School asked,
"Who knows the name of Jesus' mother?"
Everyone shouted "Mary!"
"And his father?"
One little boy said, "Verge." "Where did you
get that?" asked the nun.
"Well, They're always talking about Verge 'n'
Mary."

An Irish painter named Connery often
thinned out his paint to make it go just a bit
further. Nobody knew this and so St.
Bridget's hired him to repaint their exterior
because his bid was by far the lowest.
Connery was nearly finished with the job
when there was a clap of thunder followed
by a hard rain and all the paint washed
away.
Connery prayed hard:
"Oh sweet Mary, mother of God and all the
saints in heaven! Forgive me and tell me
what to do!"
And a mighty voice thundered:
"Repaint! Repaint! And thin no more!"

Lots O' Limericks

THE BEST OF IRISH HUMOR

There was a young man from Choctaw
Who wanted to meet Bernard Shaw.
When asked as to why,
He made no reply;
But sharpened his circular saw.

A cheese that had plenty to say
Was walking and talking one day.
Said the cheese, "Kindly note
That my Ma was a goat,
And I'm made out of curds, by the whey!"

A cute English lassie named Myrtle
Was so fecund and fruitful and fertile,
She was got with a child
By the gay Oscar Wilde,
Through a crack in her chastity girdle.

There was a young lady from Crewe
Who said, "I don't drink, I don't chew.
But do not think, therefore,
There is nothing I care for,
If you get what I mean, and you do."

A lovely young lass named Colleen
So wanted to see and be seen.
She went out in the nude
Which was terribly rude
But she gave not a hoot nor a bean.

There was a young fellow named Rice
Who remarked, "They say bigamy's nice.
Even two is a bore—
I prefer three or four,
For the plural of spouse, it is spice."

Said a maid: "I will marry for lucre."
Well, her scandalized Ma almost shucre;
But when the chance came,
And she told the old dame.
I notice she didn't rebucre.

Said a Hollywood sex queen named Mae,
"I've returned from Hawaii to stay.
The Islands are grand,
But give me a land
Where a lay is a lay, not a lei."

[360]

A Shakespearean actor named Yorick
Was able in moments euphoric
To bring to perfection
Three kinds of erection:
Corinthian, Ionic, and Doric.

There was a young lady from Ghent,
Who said she knew what it meant
When men asked her to dine,
Fed her whiskey and wine,
She knew what it meant—but she went.

'Twas said Madam Lupescu
Who came to Roumania's rescue
"It's a very nice thing
To be under a King.
Is democracy better? I ask you."

A bather whose clothing was strewed
By big winds that left her quite nude
Saw a man come along
And, unless we are wrong,
You expect this last line to be lewd.

[361]

A mouse in her room woke Miss Dowd
Who was frightened, it must be allowed.
Soon a happy thought hit her,
To scare off the critter.
She sat up in her bed and meowed.

An exceedingly fat friend of mine,
When asked at what hour he'd dine,
Replied, "At eleven,
At three, five, and seven,
And eight, and a quarter to nine."

If Jonah had just gone to Yale
Instead of the gut of a whale,
He'd have a diploma,
A better aroma,
And a nice little condo in Vail.

The limerick packs laughs anatomical
Into space that is quite economical.
But the good ones I've seen
So seldom are clean,
And the clean ones so seldom are comical.

A critic refused, as reviewer,
To read the obscene and impure.
He soon left the scene,
For the books that were clean
Just kept getting fewer and fewer.

God's plan had a hopeful beginning
But Man spoilt his chances by sinning.
We trust that the story
Will end in great glory;
But at present, the other side's winning.

An opera star named Mariah
Always tried to sing higher and higher
'Til she hit a high note
That got stuck in her throat
Now she sings with the Heavenly Choir.

If you find for your verse there's no call,
And you can't afford paper at all
For the poet true born—
However forlorn—
There's always the rest room's back wall.

There was an anthologist who
Decided that naught was taboo.
Her words are so rude,
Her verses so lewd
Sure, they'll be appealing to you.

Said a lively young nursemaid in Padua
To her master, "Please, sir, you're a
dadua.
I've come for some pins
For to wrap up your twins
And to hear you remark, sir, how gladua.

There once was a gnu in a zoo
Who tired of the same daily view.
To seek a new sight,
He stole out one night,
And where he went, gnobody gnew.

Maureen sang so well in the choir,
Her voice rose hoir and hoir,
Till it reached such a height
It was clear out of sight,
And they found it next day in the spoir.

[364]

There once was a fellow of Trinity
Who raised xyz to infinity;
And then the old brute
Extracted the root.
He afterwards took to Divinity.

A lovely young lady from Clare
Said, "I really do not have a care.
I love many men,
Kevin, Conor, and Ken,
And they are all happy to share."

A lady, an expert on skis,
Went out with a man who said, "Plis
On the next precipice
Will you give me a kice?"
She said, "Quick, before somebody sis!"

A young lassie from sweet Ballybunion
Whose kisses were sweeter than honey,
The Irishmen galore
Would line up at her door
All willing to pay her some money.

O'Hara you boast yourself handy
At selling good ale and bright brandy,
But the fact is your liquor
Makes everyone sicker—
Perhaps you should sell instead candy.

But your poems and pints, by your favour,
Are alike wholly wanting in flavour.
Because it's your pleasure,
You give us short measure—
And your ale has a ditchwater savour.

To an Irishman landing in Heaven
Said St. Peter: "We dine sharp at seven.
Then breakfast's at eight,
Never mind if you're late,
And there's Irish crubeens at eleven."

There was a young lass from Rosscarbery,
Who started to count every calorie.
Said her boss in disgust:
"If you lose half your bust,
Then you're worth only half of your salary."

A lass on the road to Goleen
Met a baker with pots of poteen.
Five minutes of lovin
Put a bun in her oven,
The next time she won't be so keen.

There was a young man from Tyrone
Who strolled by himself all alone.
He's a face like a hatchet,
I defy you to match it.
Said he: "I don't mind, it's my own."

A fellow who folks all called Barney
He wanted to visit Killarney.
He'd been told the colleens
Were all sex machines
But found that was Irishman's blarney.

In Ireland a Garda on his beat
Saw a couple more fond than discreet.
"Though a Miss, miss a kiss,
Give the next kiss a miss—
For a kiss is amiss in the street."

[367]

Two tourists at fair Salthill Strand:
They tried to make love on the sand,
The Garda on duty
Said, "No, me proud beauty,
Them foreign contortions is banned."

A young Irish lad like a giant
Was in sexual ways non-compliant.
One day he went swimming
With twelve naked women
And deserted them all for a pint.

A young Irish farmer named Billy
Whose behavior was frequently silly,
At a big farmers' ball
Dressed in nothing at all.
He claimed he came there as a filly.

A woman from sweet Donegal
Who seemed to have triplets each fall
Was asked how and wherefore?
Said, "That's what we're here for
But we often get nothing at all."

[368]

A candid young girl named McMillan
Replied to an arrogant villain
Who leered, "Now I'll rape you!"
"I cannot escape you;
But rape me you'll not, for I'm willin'."

A gorgeous voluptuous creature
Seduced a young Methodist preacher;
It worked out quite well,
For under his spell
This gal's now a Sunday school teacher.

There was a young lady from Gloucester,
Met a passionate fellow who tossed her.
She wasn't much hurt,
But he dirtied her skirt,
So think of the anguish it cost her!

When Nora was told about sex
She said, "Mother, it sounds so complex.
Do you mean you and father
Went through all that bother,
And I'm just the after-effects?"

Winter is here with his grouch,
The time when you sneeze and you slouch;
You can't take your women
Canoein' or swimmin'...
But a lot can be done on a couch.

There was a young man of high station
Who was found by a pious relation
Making love in a ditch
To—I won't say a bitch—
But a woman of NO reputation.

A lissome psychotic named Jane
Once kissed every man on a train.
Said she, "Please don't panic,
I'm just nymphomanic.
It wouldn't be fun, were I sane."

There once was a lady named Mabel
So ready, so willing, so able,
And so full of spice
She could name her own price.
Now Mabel's all wrapped up in sable.

There once was a maid with such graces
That her curves cried aloud for embraces.
"You look," said McGee,
"Like a million to me—
Invested in all the right places."

A priest read and told from his text
How Samson was scissored and vexed;
Then a barber arose
From his sweet Sunday doze
Got rattled, and shouted, "Who's next?"

You probably never have heard
Of this rather eccentric old beard
Who lived in a hole
In the ground, the poor soul,
To get used to being interred.

An Irish lass loves not her lover
So much as she loves his love of her.
Then loves she her lover
For love of her lover,
Or love of her love of her lover?

A lass near the bay of Blacksod
Thought babies were made up by God.
But 'twas not the Almighty
Who pulled up her nightie,
'Twas a clot from Killkenny, by God!

In Belfast there dwelt a sweet maid
Who swore that she wasn't afraid.
But a farmer from Derry
Came after her cherry.
'Twas not an advance, 'twas a raid!

Sure, I dine at the best spot in Cork,
On the best of pig's head and of pork.
I eat spuds and boiled eggs,
And huge turkey legs,
And I don't have to use knife or fork.

In the ancient old town of Kinsale,
Where there's lashin's of beer and of ale,
Where each man despite strife,
Lives with his own wife.
If you've heard something else, it's a tale!

A complacent old Don of Divinity
Made boast of his daughter's virginity:
"They must have been dawdling,
The students of Magdalen;
It couldn't have happened at Trinity."

I once knew a girl named O'Brien
Who taught holy hymns to a lion.
Of the lady there's some
In the lion's tum-tum.
The rest twangs a harp up in Zion.

There was a faith healer in Deal
Who said, "Although pain is not real,
When I sit on a pin
And it punctures my skin,
I dislike what I fancy I feel."

There was a young lady called Lily
With a craving to walk Picadilly.
She said, "Ain't it funny?
It's not to make money,
But men think my refusing it silly!"

A young Irish servant in Drogheda
Had a mistress who often annogheda;
Whereupon she would swear
In a language so rare
That thereafter nobody emplogheda.

There was a young lady called Maud,
A sort of society fraud;
In the parlour, I'm told
She was distant and cold,
But on the verandah, my Gawd!

There was a young lady of Joppa
Who came a society cropper;
She went to Ostend
With a gentleman friend—
And the rest of the story's improper.

Though his plan, when he gave her a buzz,
Was to do what a man always does,
She declared, "I'm a soul,
Not a sexual goal."
So he shrugged and called someone who
was.

[374]

Said Ms Murphy, on one of her larks,
"Sex is more fun in bed than in parks.
You feel more at ease,
Your behind doesn't freeze,
And passers-by don't make remarks."

There was a young lady of Kent
Who gave up her husband for Lent.
The night before Easter
When Jesus released her,
It didn't make a damn bit of difference
because in the meantime
he'd been running around
with a whole lot of other women
and she was well
and truly
screwed.

When Mammy and Da got quite plastered
And their shame had been thoroughly
mastered,
They told their boy Harry,
"Son, we never did marry.
But don't tell the neighbors, you bastard."

[375]

A fellow who made love as few can
Had a fancy to try with a toucan
He owned like a man
The collapse of his plan.
"I can't—but I bet none of *you* can."

Said an eminent, erudite ermine:
"There's one thing I cannot determine:
When a dame wears my coat
She's a person of note...
When I wear it, I'm called only vermin."

There once was a plesiosaurus
Who lived when the world was all porous.
But it fainted with shame
When it first heard its name
And departed long ago before us.

Concerning the birds, bees and flowers,
In the fields and the gardens and bowers:
You will tell at a glance
That their ways of romance
Haven't any resemblance to ours.

[376]

There was a young man named Colquhoun
Who kept as a pet a babuhoun.
His mother said, "Cholmondeley,
I don't think it's quite colmondeley,
To feed your babuhoun with a spuhoun."

There was a young farmer from Slough
Who said, "I've a terrible cough.
Do you think I should get
Both the doc and the vet
Or for now, would just one be enough?"

It is time to make love, douse the glim;
The evening sky becomes dim.
The stars will soon peep
As the birds fall asleep,
And the loin shall lie down with the limb.

There was a young fellow named Fisher
Who was fishing for fish in a fissure;
Then a cod with a grin
Pulled the fisherman in...
Now they're fishing the fissure for Fisher.

A tight-handed writer named Wright
In writing "write" always wrote "rite",
When he meant to write "write."
If he'd written "write" right,
Wright would not have wrought rot writing
"rite."

She frowned and called him "Mr"
Because in sport he kr;
And so, in spite,
That very night,
The Mr kr sr.

There was an old man in a hearse,
Who murmured, "This might have been
worse;
Of course the expense
Is simply immense.
But it doesn't come out of <u>my</u> purse."

I sell the best brandy and sherry
To make my good customers merry;
But at times their finances
Run short as it chances,
And then I feel very sad, very.

[378]

A farmer from Newcastlewest
Who courted a maiden with zest,
So hard did he press her
To make her say, "Yes, sir,"
That he broke the ould watch in his vest.

A lassie from this side of Rathmore
Was wed to one hell of a bore...
A dopey old farmer
Too lazy to warm her
All he did every night was just snore.

A lovely young lassie from Crosser
Who in spiritual things was a messer
When sent to the priest,
This lewd little beast,
Did her best to seduce her confessor.

Oh I'd love to live near Adrigole
And draw fifty a week on the dole,
And to hear the birds sing
And the waterfall ring
And a big cozy fire of free coal.

A pretty young lass from Kilquane
While walking was caught in the rain.
She ran—almost flew—
Her complexion did too!
And she reached home exceedingly plain.

There is a creator named God
Whose doings are sometimes quite odd.
He made Kerrymen cute,
Tipperarymen mute
Which when all's said and done is just cod!

A young lass on the fair stand of Howe
Said sadly she didn't know how.
Then an Irishman caught her
And bloody soon taught her,
And did it without any row.

A tourist just near Dunamark
When he made love, he just had to bark.
His wife was a bitch
With a terrible itch.
Now the town cannot sleep after dark!

There was a young woman from Potts
Who, when learning Morse Code, cried out,
"What's the matter with me?
Dashes fill me with glee—
But I can't get along with the dots!"

A well-endowed lady from Bude
Went swimming one day in the nude.
From the lifeguard a shout:
"All inflatibles out!"
There was no need to be quite so rude.

A lass from the County of Down
Observed that the sea was so calm
"I'll swim out for a lark."
Well, she met a large shark
Let us now sing the 90th Psalm.

There was a young poet of Kew
Who failed to emerge into view.
So he said, "I'll dispense
With rhyme, meter, and sense."
And he did, and he's now in Who's Who.

[381]

Said St. Joan on the pile, "I confess
To be burned at the stake is a mess.
Though I frankly avow
I'm smoking more now,
But clearly enjoying it less."

I'm saying me prayers to St. Jude
To keep away thoughts that are lewd.
He'll do what he can
To get me a man
And we'll wed, and we'll bed; is that rude?

A young man near the Bridge of Blackwater
Who daily got shorter and shorter,
"The reason," he said
"Is the brains in me head
Get so heavy that I fear a disorder."

In old Wicklow some visitors will go
To see what no person should know.
But then there are tourists—
The purest of purists—
Who say 'tis uncommonly low!

[382]

Said a girl making love in a shanty:
"My dear, your legs are all slanty."
    He replied: "I can use
    Any angle I choose.
I do as I please—I'm from Bantry!"

There was a great lord in Japan
Whose name on a Tuesday began.
    It carried through Sunday
    Till twilight on Monday,
And sounded like stones in a can.

A dentist named Archibald Moss
Fell in love with the toothsome Miss Ross
    But he held in abhorrence
    Her Christian name, Florence,
So he named her his own Dental Floss.

There once was a bonny Scotch laddie
Who said as he put on his plaidie,
    "I've just had a dish
    O' unco' guid fish."
What had he had? Had he had haddie?

[383]

There was a young girl called Bianca
Who slept while her ship lay at anchor;
She awoke with dismay
When she heard the mate say:
"Hi! Hoist up the top sheet and spanker!"

A mortician who practiced in Fife
Made love to the corpse of his wife.
"How could I know, judge.
She was cold, did not budge—
Just the same as she'd been all her life."

A spinster who came from Donmoor
Was grasped by a vulgar young boor.
This detestable varmint
Unfastened her garment,
But proved to be just a voyeur.

A bibulous bishop would preach
After sunning himself on the beach.
But his love life was ended
By a paunch so distended
It annulled, *ipso facto*, his reach.

"I'm a hardware store clerk," said Miss
Hughes,
"But some kinds of work I refuse.
I'll handle their nuts,
Their bolts and cross cuts,
But I simply will not hand out screws."

A certain young fellow named Hector
Slyly said to a girl as he necked he,
"Do you very much care
If I pull out some hair?
You see, I'm a box-top collector.

Said a groom to his amorous mate,
"My dear, I'm afraid you must wait.
For whatever comes next
I must study the text—
It's continued on page eighty-eight."

A pious young lady named Finegan
Would caution a friend, "Now you're in
again.
Please do time it right,
Make it last through the night,
For I really do not want to sin again."

A virgin emerged from her bath
In a state of right righteous wrath,
For she'd been deflowered
When she bent as she showered,
And the handle was right in the path.

The play about Oedipus Rex
Has a plot that is very complex.
He clobbered his paw,
Then screwed his own maw
While the chorus sang songs about sex.

A braw Scottish soldier named Rex
Abstains from all manner of sex.
He's more than a Spartan.
Because of his tartan
He suffers from kiltie complex.

A fearless young spermatozoa
Remarked to an ovum, "Helloa!
We'd make a cute fetus,
But I fear she'd mistreat us.
By the looks of this place, she's a whoah."

There was a young lady of Wheeling
Said to her beau, "I've a feeling
My little brown jug
Has need of a plug."
And straightaway started to peeling.

A gardening nut from O'Hare
Grew apples and grapes in his hair.
One day on the beach
He met a young peach
Now the peach and the nut are a pear.

In the Garden of Eden was Adam
Disporting himself with his madam.
She was filled with elation
For in all of creation
There was only one man and she had 'im.

There was a young lady from Pace
Whose corsets would no longer lace.
Her mother said, "Nelly
There's more in your belly
Then ever went in through your face."

An old couple living in Gloucester
Had a beautiful girl but they loucester.
She fell from a yacht
And never the spacht
Could be found where the cold waves had
toucester.

An unpopular youth in Cologne
With a pain in his stomach did mogne.
He heaved a great sigh
And said, "I would digh
But the loss would be only my ogne.

In Ireland two people of taste
Were beautiful down to the waist.
So they limited love
To the regions above
And thus remained perfectly chaste.

There was a youn
g maid from Madras
Who had a magnificent ass.
Not rounded and pink
As you probably think.
It was gray, had long ears, and ate grass.

There was a young curate in Kew
Who kept his pet cat in a pew.
He taught it to speak
Alphabetical Greek.
But it never got further than Mu.

A kindly old harlot from China
Declared, "I have never felt finer.
And so poor men won't holler,
I'll charge them just one dollar
And 25 cents for a minor."

There once was a peasant named Gorse
Who fell madly in love with a horse.
Said his wife, "You rapscallion,
The horse is a stallion—
This constitutes grounds for divorce!"

A king sadly said to his queen,
"In parts, you have grown far from lean."
"I don't give a damn,
You've always liked ham,"
She replied, and he gasped, "How obscene!"

[389]

There are some things we mustn't expose
So we hide them away in our clothes.
Oh, it's shocking to stare
At what's certainly there—
But why this is so, heaven knows.

There was a young lady of Spain
Who took down her pants on the train.
There was a young porter
Saw more than he orter
And asked her to do it again.

Said a calendar model named Gloria,
"So the men can enjoy real euphoria,
You pose as you are,
In Jan Feb and Mar,
Then in April they want to see Moria."

There's a singer in Donegal city
Whose form is impressively pretty;
She is often addressed
By the name of 'Beau Chest'
Which is thought to be tasteful and witty.

[390]

A girl who was from Brooklyn Heights
Looked quite mediocre in tights.
There was much more approval
When upon their removel
She revealed more spectacular sights.

There was a young woman named Astor
Whose clothes fitted tight as a plaster.
When she happened to sneeze
She felt a cold breeze
And knew she had met with disaster.

A virgin from County of Clare
Would do any old thing on a dare.
But one dare, she found
Made her tummy grow round,
And she now has a visitor there.

Said an ovum one night to a sperm,
"You're a very attractive young germ!
Come join me, my sweet,
Let our nuclei meet
And in nine months we'll both come to
term."

[391]

Write your own limericks here.

.

THE BEST OF IRISH HUMOR